TEXT BY

CHIARA PASQUALETTI JOHNSON

ILLUSTRATIONS BY

ALESSANDRO VENTRELLA

INTRODUCTION

This book is an invitation to dream big, to overturn stereotypes, to speak up and break down prejudices. But above all, it is an invitation to roll up your sleeves and take control of your own destiny, aiming straight for a bright future where everyone can be free to fulfill their dreams. Just as the protagonists of these pages did. We selected 50 women, but there could have been 100 or 1,000. Nonconformist, imaginative, pioneering, and fearless, they are the faces of a revolution destined to change stereotypes forever and impose gender equality in all fields. Eccentric, bold, and courageous, they are neither princesses nor saints. They are genuine people, full of contradictions and beautifully imperfect. Sweet but determined, they represent the infinite shades of the same values. Like contemporary muses, they inspire objectives, anticipate progress, create futures. With different spirits, they all tell a single story, the story of a generation that is leading change, thus making us imagine the world to come. They prove by their example that it is possible to get out of the ordinary and turn our life into a marvelous parable. By cultivating their talent, they chose to become rock stars, rescue human lives, found startups, or even save the planet. But once they reached their goal, they did not stop. "We cannot simply be successful when half of us are left behind," they told themselves. "If what I do is just useful for myself, then it's not enough. It has to be useful for us all, or rather for everyone." And so, they turned their experiences and

achievements into a powerful encouragement by sharing resources, acts, actions, and words.

With their lives and feats, they picked up the baton from their grandmothers and great-grandmothers who made it possible for the society of the past century to grow and evolve, thus improving the status of women and significantly contributing to provide everyone with rights and awareness. We owe a great deal to the generations of rebel young women who in the past had to elbow their way into a patriarchal society, paving the way for those who followed them. I dedicated *The Most Influential Women of Our Time* (White Star, 2018) to the brave warriors of the 20th century. It collects the stories of the heroines who stood out for their strong character and tenacity all over the world. By studying their lives, I learned to recognize and admire those who have the courage to change the rules of the game. Today it is the responsibility of a new generation, my generation, and the story that was interrupted at the end of that book ideally continues in these pages and pays tribute to today's girls. This book is dedicated to them, and I hope that these stories will not be read only by women, but also by men, because the fight against stereotypes must start from a cultural shift that implies that we must stop teaching boys and girls that the world is all pink or blue, or that there still exists "man stuff." How many young girls hear that when they want to study scientific subjects? It will be a great day when it does not count anymore if a woman or a man manages to achieve success, or power, or simply the freedom to choose whom to be. It is a goal that seems distant today, given that every female achievement still makes the news, and it seems that there is something quite extraordinary in a woman leader who prevails in a man's world. Because if it is true that women are already strong, then it is a matter of changing the way the world perceives that strength.

The attitude toward equality is evolving, but even the youngest generation is not immune to stereotypes and gender disparities. Today, the gender gap is still felt, especially in the workplace, and it is a gross mistake because now more than ever it is the strength of women that reflects that of a country. It is just as dangerous being tempted to consider them as a separate, fragile category that must be protected because in this way we end up triggering a rivalry that risks setting the male and female universes against each other. Nothing could be more wrong, because the more women work and get quality jobs, the more the system thrives, and employment opportunities increase for everyone. But there is more: in a world that, out of prejudice, allows only half of the population to stand out, the best personalities certainly cannot emerge. How many potential female musicians, writers, stateswomen, inventors, or explorers did we miss over the centuries because women could neither study nor work? And yet, even today, millions of young girls are kept out of the picture even if they are full of unexpressed potential or, worse, full of a potential repressed by a society that is certainly not structured to their measure. That's why stories like that of Abisoye Ajayi-Akinfolarin, who teaches coding to young Nigerian slum girls, or like that of Fatoumata Kébé, who reveals the secrets of the universe to young students from the Parisian banlieue, are exemplar. Equally powerful are the stories of female artists who are giving a voice to change, or of the courageous activists whose lives have been destroyed by the violence of war or of a crazy climate, like Amani Ballour and Xiye Bastida, who both fight for young boys and girls from all over the world. Each of them has different stories and ideas, but they all share the same determination and will to fight on the front lines for the right to education, to protect "our house on fire" due to climate change, or to guarantee all children the right to go to school safely. Their stories are interwoven with intelligence, talent, brilliance, and grace, but also with that special beauty that makes every person unique. Because having an appearance different from all the people surrounding us and understanding that this, too, is a power we need to explore is part of the revolution.

Bound together by an invisible network, the lives of the protagonists of this book are occasionally intertwined with one another, bringing out the common threads that connect some of these stories. As in the case of the humanitarian commitment that took Nadia Murad to meet her lawyer Amal Ramzi Alamuddin, of the special bond represented by a gold ring that Oprah Winfrey gave to Amanda Gorman, of the mutual admiration between Malala Yousafzai and Emma Watson, of the T-shirts that Maria Grazia Chiuri paraded on Dior's catwalk with the message "We should all be feminists" (a quotation from the Nigerian writer Chimamanda Ngozi Adichie) printed on them, and finally of the portraits by Annie Leibovitz, who photographed many of these women, enhancing the femininity of every body and face. By their example, they handed over the keys of power to millions of women, opening doors that had remained locked for far too long and showing that there are no such things as pipe dreams. "It's not me who has to change, but the world around me," they repeat to themselves. By reading their stories, you will rediscover known and well-known personalities, but you will also find unexpected heroines who, by the end of your reading, will leave you with only two words on the tip of your tongue: thank you. Thank you for your courage, for having made it, and for continuing to fight. Because when we see a dream that comes true, we all believe a little more in our own dream.

CHIMAMANDA NGOZI ADICHIE

Feminism, femininity, politics, racism, and blackness are some of the topics that this writer holds dear. She believes that the real goal of feminism is to become an obsolete movement so as to move forward once and for all in the name of equality.

"We should all be feminists" is her most famous quote. It spread like a mantra, printed on Dior T-shirts and repeated in chorus at Beyoncé's concerts. It then became the title of a book already considered a classic, so much so that in Sweden it was handed out for free to all sixteen-year-olds. An amazing orator, Chimamanda uttered this sentence during one of the TED Talks that made her famous and known as an activist, turning her into a point of reference for the world public opinion. "After that unexpected success I felt I had a responsibility to keep talking about it, even if it means having less time to do what I love most: writing and reading."

WE DON'T NEED TO BE PERFECT TO DO WHAT'S RIGHT.

Her writing skills led her to literary success with titles such as *Purple Hibiscus, Half of a Yellow Sun,* and *Americanah.* However, her messages are not only conveyed through the pages of her books. In fact, one of Chimamanda's many talents is to be able to adapt to every kind of platform. "If you use different media, you can talk about more things you care about, and people will listen to you." Always impeccably dressed, made-up, and with beautiful hairstyles, she chose to use Instagram to promote Nigerian fashion, which she wears in each of her portraits. She has a natural predisposition for elegance, which she manages to turn into an ideological stance. "That a woman, to be taken seriously, has to give up taking care of herself is an entirely Western idea. It dates back to when the first activists began to cut their hair and deny their femininity to overturn the idea of the woman as an object/property of her husband. It made sense back then, today it doesn't. When success came, I decided to reclaim the opportunity to express my femininity and get interested in fashion without fear of being considered frivolous. Just as a man who is passionate about engines is not considered frivolous. I did it for myself, but also in the hope that younger girls, seeing me, will find the courage to do the same."

For her, the uniqueness of each human being is a treasure, and the difference between men and women should not be denied, nor should it be used as an instrument of power and submission, as she points out in all of her public speeches. "I never thought of becoming a feminist icon, it was not my intention: I am a writer, literature is the love of my life. But even as a child I was angry about the difference in treatment between me and my male peers," she said in an interview. She referred to the value of differences also while speaking about her life between two cultures, since she is Nigerian by birth but American by choice. Chimamanda has chosen to reside part of the year in Lagos and the other part in the United States. "I don't consider myself an immigrant, but a very lucky person with two homes, two citizenships, and two points of view. Identity has always been a complex issue, and paradoxically it is even better that it becomes more so in such a mobile world."

NEVER EVER ACCEPT "BECAUSE YOU ARE A WOMAN" AS A REASON FOR DOING OR NOT DOING ANYTHING.

ABISOYE AJAYI-AKINFOLARIN

They call her the Coding Hero. Her mission is to teach Nigerian girls and make them love computer science and technology so as to give them the chance to plan a different future for themselves, away from slums and poverty.

Abisoye's childhood in Nigeria was not easy. She did not have a mother to look after her, and her father was abusive. "I know what it feels like to be from an underserved community. I know what it feels like to be a vulnerable young girl," she said. Then, when she was ten, her brother took her to an Internet café, where she first discovered computers. With her fingers flying on the keyboard, she studied computer science and she tested her skills rising through the ranks of high-tech startups in Lagos, the Nigerian Silicon Valley where giants such as Facebook and Google are headquartered.

MY **GIRLS** ARE **CODERS.**
THEY ARE **THINKERS.**
THEIR FUTURE IS **BRIGHT.**

"Technology gave me a voice, as well as economic independence, and I feel that it's a path that someone from a disadvantaged background can take to find success in life." That's why she quit a full-time job and she created the Pearls Africa Foundation, an association that aims to help the poorest young girls to reach their potential through computer science. "Girls are lacking in the STEM industries, so I was angry with what was going on, and I wanted to turn things around." So, in 2015, she launched the GirlsCoding project, which aims to teach teenage girls living in internally displaced people camps, orphanages, or correctional homes how to code and develop software, smartphone apps, and websites. It is an ambitious project whose goal is to train young female programmers for the Nigerian high-tech industry, but above all to prevent many of them from becoming teenage mothers. "Any free time girls from underserved communities get, they can get pregnant. But if their confidence level can come from the fact that they are programmers, then hopefully it can improve their entire life," she explained.

Many of these girls had never seen a computer before, but all of them gained the self-confidence they needed to change their lives by acquiring the technical knowledge required to find a job. In addition to practical training, the program also includes visits to high-tech industries so that students can picture themselves working in those environments one day, because, according to Abisoye, "empowering these young women with experience in the STEM fields automatically increases the probability that they can transcend the conditions of poverty they currently exist in." She believes that computer science gave equal opportunities to young, disadvantaged Africans. It is possible to make up for years of poor-quality instruction and precarious living conditions with a coding course, and those opportunities that were once available only to graduates coming from the most prestigious universities suddenly become open to everyone, including slum girls. "I believe you can still find diamonds in these places. They need to be shown another life."

MARGARET ATWOOD

A visionary, multi-award-winning, and almost prophetic writer, Margaret Atwood is an activist in her own way, and she declares loudly and on paper her support for women, the environment, and freedom.

The red cloaks worn by the protagonists of her most famous novel have become a symbol of feminism all over the world. She herself is considered one of the quintessential feminist writers. And yet, when asked if she defines herself as such, her answer is: "It depends on what is meant by feminism." If one implies that women are better than men, then she doesn't agree. Women are a part of humanity, and Margaret has always supported the rights of human beings, all of them. With her high cheekbones, fair complexion, and gray hair framing her head like a crown, she is a queen of literature.

I HOPE THAT PEOPLE WILL FINALLY COME TO REALIZE THAT THERE IS ONLY ONE "RACE" – THE HUMAN RACE – AND THAT WE ARE ALL MEMBERS OF IT.

A two-time winner of the Booker Prize and nominated several times for the Nobel Prize, Margaret has written novels, poetry collections, nonfiction books, dozens of short stories, fairy tales for children, and even graphic novels. However, she is especially famous for *The Handmaid's Tale*, a novel in which she tells the status of women in a dystopic future dominated by a misogynist theocracy that imposes the isolation of women, the veiling, and the obligation of having children. Maybe because some writers are able to see more forward than normal people, one gets the impression that those lines were written today, even if more than thirty years have passed since the first publication of this book. As she herself explained to the *New York Times,* "My women suffer because most of the women I talk to seem to have suffered." If we think about Afghan women, Margaret Atwood's novel is almost prophetic, even if she says the opposite, with her usual irony. "Nobody is really able to predict the future, we can guess, build hypothesis. If I were a prophet I would have cleaned up on the stock market years ago."

With the same clear look on things that has always guided her, Margaret continues to travel around the world collecting awards as a writer, but also supporting campaigns to prevent multinationals from destroying the ecosystems. She never shied away from public exposure or from getting her hands dirty, and not just for global issues. Since she grew up surrounded by the Canadian wilderness and her father was an entomologist, she has always been a defender of the environment in all its nuances, even if she does not like to be labeled as an activist: "I am a writer, and as such I find myself describing certain realities. I am an activist by chance." She writes articles and signs open letters for the causes she supports: Greta Thunberg's environmentalism, freedom of speech, women, and LGBTQ+ rights. "I was brought up like this: to listen and respect who I am in front of, no matter who they are." Just as the heroines of her novels, who react to adversities and get organized to fight them, she decided to never give up. According to Margaret, there is still much to write. And to do.

WE STILL THINK OF A POWERFUL MAN AS A BORN LEADER AND A POWERFUL WOMAN AS AN ANOMALY.

AMANI BALLOUR

Courage, resilience, empathy, and compassion are the extraordinary qualities characterizing this pediatrician who ran an underground hospital in Syria for two years. Her heroic feat has been documented in an Oscar-nominated movie, so that no one can say "I didn't know it."

A few miles from Damascus, in the ruins of a city destroyed by bombing, the sick and injured were treated in a secret underground hospital known as "The Cave." Operating rooms and hospital wards were linked to all the different areas of the city by means of labyrinthine tunnels and dank and dark corridors. Here, Dr. Amani Ballour, a young doctor specializing in pediatrics who was forced to abandon her studies when the war in Syria broke out, used to work around the clock. "When the situation got out of hand I decided to stay, giving priority to those lives which could be saved, and especially rescuing children. We were few doctors and none of us was prepared to witness such scenes."

I JUST WANTED TO STUDY AND BE A DOCTOR, AND HAVE A CLINIC. THAT WAS MY DREAM.

Her words reveal the suffering of someone who witnessed unspeakable horrors, situations for which no university course can really prepare. The medical and nursing staff used to work under the deafening noise of bombs and under appalling conditions, in poky and crowded clinics, where medicines and food were scarce and the patients to treat were far too many. When her colleagues elected Amani as head of the hospital, she was less than thirty years old. During the following two years, she worked tirelessly, dealing every day with fear and sorrow, but also with the sexism and patriarchal conservatism of many of her patients. "They used to tell me: 'We need a man for this kind of job, not you,' 'Women should stay at home,' 'Aren't there any male doctors in the area?' And still others refused to talk to me saying that they would only talk to male doctors." And so, when the director Feras Fayyad contacted her proposing to document her work at the hospital and make a movie, she decided to accept. "I refused at the beginning, it was too dangerous, but then I realized the importance of the project. I got to the point where I was afraid that I was going to die and so I thought it would be useful to leave this sort of legacy." The documentary called *The Cave* won plenty of awards and was nominated for an Oscar, bringing a harsh but necessary denunciation on the big screen. It shows without filters the siege, the hunger, the use of chemical weapons, but also the status of women in a conservative society that oppresses them, forcing them to team up. "I always try to support women. I hope that we will soon be able to obtain the rights to which we are entitled and to achieve true equality between men and women," said Amani. In March 2018, the umpteenth bombing rendered the underground hospital unusable, and she was forced to flee with a heavy heart to save herself. She currently lives far from her country, but her human and professional commitment continues. With the help of the King Baudouin Foundation, she created Al Amal (which means "hope"), an organization that supports women committed to running hospitals and emergency departments in conflict zones. For her courage, Amani was awarded the Council of Europe's Raoul Wallenberg Prize, which rewards humanitarian activities, with this motivation: "Human rights and personal dignity are not a peacetime luxury. Dr. Amani Ballour is a shining example of the empathy, virtue, and honor that can flourish even in the worst circumstances: in the midst of war and suffering."

I DON'T WANT TO TELL STORIES TO MAKE PEOPLE CRY AND GET UPSET, I WANT THEM TO HELP.

XIYE BASTIDA

Her indigenous roots taught her to take care of Mother Earth. After experiencing the effects of climate change firsthand, she leads a new generation of young environmentalists with energy, optimism, and glee.

Her name in the language of the ancient Central American people of Otomi means "soft rain," and it was precisely rain that turned this young Mexican girl into a climate justice activist. Her story began in San Pedro Tultepec, not far from Mexico City, where weeks of torrential rainfall turned streets into rivers. Xiye was only fifteen when her home was destroyed by violent floods caused by climate change. "As I was growing up, the eternal snowed-peaked volcano in the valley I was born—the Toluca Valley—began to gradually lose its whiteness," she recalls.

BY 2050, I WILL BE 48 YEARS OLD, AND WHEN I LOOK OUT OF THE WINDOW, I WILL SEE THE WORLD YOU ARE NEGOTIATING RIGHT NOW.

The devastating effects of crazy weather prompted her parents, both environmentalists, to move to the United States, where Xiye had to start from scratch by learning a new language and carving out a role for herself in a society that was completely different from the one she came from. "I was raised with philosophies that my dad learned throughout his life, like reciprocity to Mother Earth, which basically means that everything we need to survive and thrive, Mother Earth gives us. And all they ask is that we protect it." Xiye did not know where to start, so she decided to join the school's environmental club, where she found her voice. She immediately felt in tune with the young people of the Sunrise Movement, with the non-violent activists of Extinction Rebellion, and with Fridays for Future, of which she became one of the best-known faces.

On September 20, 2019, she led the greatest global protest of the movement in the streets of New York, and she welcomed Greta Thunberg in Manhattan. Today, Xiye divides her time between university studies and environmental commitment. "The world is so big, and it has so many bad habits," she said during her TED Talk.

At the age of nineteen, she founded the environmental association Re-Earth Initiative, and she was the only activist who spoke at the climate summit held in 2021 for World Environment Day.

Age does not seem to matter in Xiye's life, and her voice certainly did not shake during the video call with forty global leaders that included Xi Jinping, Putin, Merkel, and Bolsonaro. "We are not saying 'it was your fault.' We are saying that we are aware of what is happening, and we need you," she explained, thus overcoming the conflict between young people and adults to turn it into a multigenerational campaign. "We need adults. They have the voting power. They can use democracy to save our future."

With her fearless character, she is the perfect example of a new generation of climate activists who fight with a smile and no anger.

"We are a youth movement and, therefore, we try to do all this with fun and joy, in a supportive and inclusive way, to create a space where we respect each other and feel safe."

BEYONCÉ

A singer, model of body positivity, and businesswoman, Queen B, as she has been nicknamed by her fans, defends her authentic and out-of-the-traditional-canons beauty. "No one can define me," she proudly says, encouraging everyone to get free from homogenization.

The most Grammy Award–winning artist of all time is not only a singer, businesswoman, actress, and dancer, but she is also a wife and a mother. Beyoncé is all these things together, and perhaps she is even more. "My life is a journey. It seems like I set a goal and some kind of way I accomplish it, and then I set another one," she said with tears streaming down her face in the documentary *Homecoming*, which recounts her life behind the scenes of her concerts. In forty years, Beyoncé Giselle Knowles has reached the top of the BBC's list of the most powerful women in the music industry, achieving success with hard work and sacrifice. At the age of seven, she used to participate in dance competitions, at nine years old she started taking singing lessons, and by the age of ten she had already recorded at least fifty songs.

BEING "NUMBER ONE" IS NO LONGER MY PRIORITY. MY TRUE WIN IS CREATING ART AND A LEGACY THAT WILL LIVE FAR BEYOND ME.

She released her first album when she was fifteen, and at the age of twenty-two, she was already a global star. Meanwhile, she married the rapper Jay-Z, and when asked what is the title that makes her happiest of all those she has been given, she answers with no hesitation: "Being the mother of Blue, Rumi, and Sir." Motherhood also changed her relationship with a body far from those standards that have dominated the show business for far too long. She never kept it a secret that she felt a lot of pressure. "I embraced being curvier. I accepted what my body wanted to be. I think it's important for women and men to see and appreciate the beauty in their natural bodies," she told *Vogue*. Taking advantage of her immense popularity, she has put all her efforts into major social issues, taking positions against racial and gender discrimination. Inclusion and diversity are the issues she has always promoted and stood up for. "For me, it is about amplifying the beauty in all of us. I rarely felt represented in film, fashion, and other media. I made it my mission to use my art to show the style, elegance, and attraction in men and women of color." In the last ten years of her career, Beyoncé has become more and more active in the political sphere, by bringing into her music the ideas of female writers such as Chimamanda Ngozi Adichie and Audre Lorde. "Your queerness is beautiful, your blackness is beautiful. Your compassion, your understanding, your fight for people who may be different from you, is beautiful. I hope you continue to go into the world and show them that you will never stop being yourself. That it's your time now, make them see you. Diversity and inclusion go beyond race." It is a message that puts the spotlight also on women's rights and emancipation. "To the young women, our future leaders, know that you're about to make the world turn. I see you. You are everything the world needs. Make those power moves. Be excellent." Even on Instagram, she is unique: she posts a few photos strictly without captions, and never posts stories. Her being private on social media, and her choice to carefully select the public events to attend, are the result of experiences she had firsthand. "There were things in my career that I did because I didn't understand that I could say no. We all have more power than we realize," said Queen B, giving her fans yet another pearl of empowerment.

YOUR SELF-WORTH IS DETERMINED BY YOU. YOU DON'T HAVE TO DEPEND ON SOMEONE TELLING YOU WHO YOU ARE.

INNA BRAVERMAN

While the world is trying to act on climate change, the "lady of the waves" has always been at the forefront. Shortly after she was born, she nearly died from Chernobyl radiation, but she got a second chance, and she decided to devote her life to green energy.

Few entrepreneurs have a story as extraordinary as Inna's. At just twenty-four years old and with no experience whatsoever in engineering, she launched an intelligent and low-cost technology that harnesses the power of ocean waves to produce clean energy. This in itself is already impressive, but her human experience is no less remarkable because no one better than Inna can understand the devastating consequences that polluting energy sources can have. Born in Ukraine in 1986, she stopped breathing and she nearly died when the Chernobyl nuclear power plant exploded two weeks after she was born. "My mother found me lifeless in my crib and I was clinically dead. Thankfully she was a nurse and managed to resuscitate me. I was given a second chance in life," she recounted.

PASSION IS THE GREATEST RENEWABLE ENERGY SOURCE.

When she was four, her family migrated to Israel, where Inna eventually continued her studies in political science and English literature at the University of Haifa. It was while she was working as a translator in Tel Aviv at a renewable energy company that she got passionate about the idea of exploring the potential of that blue expanse she used to look at every day. "I grew up by the beach in Israel watching the ocean." Two-thirds of the world population live, like her, along the coasts and, according to the World Energy Council, ocean waves can provide twice the electricity our planet needs. Thus, when she met the Canadian surfer David Leb, the two came up with the idea of harnessing the ocean energy by using a simple but smart system made of buoys hanging from already existing artificial structures like piers or jetties, thus simplifying the placement, maintenance, and accessibility of the system. In 2011, she created the Eco Wave Power company.

Shortly after, the first power plant was inaugurated in the port of Jaffa, Israel. The same model has been replicated in other parts of the world and has proved extremely effective and environmentally friendly. "Unlike off-shore installations, we don't put cables on the ocean floor, which disrupts marine life." Her company was listed on the NASDAQ Stockholm stock exchange, and Inna has been named one of the thirty most influential women in the world by the prestigious MSN list, together with Michelle Obama and Oprah Winfrey. *Wired* magazine recognized her as one of the Females Changing the World, and she has been awarded the Global Climate Action Award by the UN. Her work has been documented by the short film *Female Planet*, made by Google in recognition of her commitment to changing the world, one wave at a time.

THIS IS SOMETHING THAT IS IMPORTANT FOR US AND FOR OUR CHILDREN AND FOR OUR CHILDREN'S CHILDREN, THE WAY THAT WE LEAVE THE WORLD FOR THEM.

MARIA GRAZIA CHIURI

Thanks to her, Dior's catwalk has become a platform of dialogue on the new role of women. She is the Italian fashion designer who is redefining the rules of the fashion world with feminism, pragmatism, and dynamism.

Her passion for fashion is at the service of women. To bring them to the center of history, she uses catwalks to put the spotlight on issues she holds dear, shaking up expectations with choices that go against the tide. Like when she presented a collection of T-shirts with titles of feminist essays printed on them: *"Why Have There Been No Great Women Artists?"* by Linda Nochlin, and *"We Should All Be Feminists"* by the activist Chimamanda Ngozi Adichie. "I did that for two reasons. First, because we have forgotten the struggles for emancipation that took place in the past. In fact, the world is dangerously moving backwards. Second, because I want to use the catwalks to support what I believe in, to promote ideas and people I'm interested in. Fashion has a great power and audience."

FASHION, LIKE ART, CAN BE A POWERFUL DEVICE FOR BREAKING THE DOMINANT CULTURAL AND VISUAL PATTERNS.

With her platinum hair, her almost always black outfits, and with a very few accessories, Maria Grazia Chiuri has been included in the annual *Financial Times'* prestigious ranking of the ten most influential women in the world. And yet, she said that fame is not for her. "I embody the most uncool fashion designer ever: I am fifty-seven, I have two sons, and I'm married." She built her career one step at a time, cultivating a passion that was born when she used to watch her mother working in her tailor shop in Rome. She took her first steps into the fashion world at Fendi, then she put her talent at the service of Valentino, and finally she arrived in Paris as creative director of the brand that invented the "new look": Christian Dior. Fashion magazines proclaimed her "an Italian on the French throne." When she debuted on the catwalk, she split the audience in half, putting in the front row not only celebrities but also modern-day heroines, writers, artists, and examples of resilience. "I chose the example of fencers such as Bebe Vio to clarify something about women once and for all: stop looking for fairy tales." She shows humility because even if she knows she achieved great things, she does not want to take all the credit for it since, as she repeatedly stated, "every project stems from a creative process of a team of people." She loves to collaborate with contemporary artists so as to turn fashion shows into a powerful device for breaking dominant cultural and visual patterns. Her objective? "Turning fashion into a vehicle through which we can build a real world, a world of multifaceted women who are beautiful because they are imperfect," she said in an interview with the magazine *Madame Le Figaro*. "Whenever I'm asked if I'm a political fashion designer, I always say yes because everything we do in our life is political." As Dior's creative director, she was honored the Legion D'Onore, the highest honor that can be bestowed by the French Republic. "I am perfectly aware of working in a market that is contested by feminism. But I'm also aware that we all live in a capitalist system. I prefer to try to improve the world of fashion from within."

MISTY COPELAND

She was a "pretty much homeless" child, and now she is the étoile of the American Ballet Theatre in New York. She is a genuine black swan, and she won her battle against poverty and prejudice with her smiles and pirouettes.

She is five feet tall with an athletic physique, and she broke the stereotypes of classical ballet: "It's important for me to send a clear message, to set an example of what a healthy image is, what a ballerina can be. That she doesn't have to be a white woman that is really thin. She could look like any woman in the world." With her achievements, Misty dismantled all barriers of race one by one by challenging prejudices. "It's just something that's so engrained in the ballet culture, in us as dancers that you just envision a certain type of person portraying that role, so it's incredible to be able to be a brown swan," she said in an interview for the BBC, thus wiping out in a second centuries of aesthetic canons that only allowed heavenly and almost anorexic ballerinas with a "peeled-apple-colored" skin in the first rows.

At the age of seventeen, thanks to a scholarship, she began her career in the American Ballet Theatre, where she was accepted as a student, and she forged ahead entering the corps de ballet and becoming principal dancer in 2015. Times are changing, but Misty still remains an exception. "I wasn't quite prepared to be the only African American at the American Ballet Theatre over the last two decades," she said during a TV show. "The realization that there are very few Black people in the world's top ballet companies was the biggest shock I have had to deal with in my career. I believe that more diversity is needed in all areas, on stage, among the audience, in the direction, and that new generations should be encouraged in this sense."

She has surely done her part by dancing in a Disney movie, posing for the Pirelli Calendar, and inspiring a Barbie doll dressed in the same red costume she wore in *Firebird*, in her first starring role. She is the embodiment of a dream, and the idol of African American young girls looking for role models in a still-too-white society.

ALL YOU CAN DO IS BE YOUR BEST SELF. I'M REPRESENTING MORE THAN JUST ME. I THINK EVERYONE SHOULD BE LIKE THAT.

SAMANTHA CRISTOFORETTI

Two lives may not be enough to put together a curriculum vitae like hers. With her steely character, titanium nerves, and high-tech heart, "AstroSamantha" shares her space adventures with the world to encourage young girls to try to fulfill their dreams.

It takes ninety minutes for the International Space Station to orbit Earth. "You never have a complete view of the whole planet. So, you see a piece of it every time, but when you go all the way around it, it's like hugging all humanity." This is how "AstroSamantha," as she has been nicknamed, speaks of the emotion of watching Earth from space. It is the same emotion she felt as a child when she used to stargaze among the Italian Alps summits. "Growing up in the mountains means seeing the sky up close. I remember its presence in my childhood nights," she says. Since then, she literally took flight to fulfill her dream with an unshakable determination.

WOMEN OFTEN TELL THEMSELVES: I'M NOT GOOD ENOUGH, NO ONE WILL TAKE ME SERIOUSLY. BUT IT'S NOT TRUE. LOOK AT ME.

With two degrees and a qualification from the Euro-NATO Joint Jet Pilot Training achieved in Texas, Samantha is licensed to pilot various kinds of aircraft. In addition to Italian, she is fluent in German, French, English, and Russian. She is Commander and Knight Grand Cross of the Order of Merit of the Italian Republic. Moreover, she holds a unique record, since, according to all surveys, Samantha is the ideal female role model for most young girls in Italy, although she minimizes it: "An astronaut is not a genius, but one who knows how to adapt anywhere and can do a bit of everything." Modest but straightforward, in 2009 she joined the crews of the European Space Agency as one of the six best applicants among 8,500 people, even if she was very close to failing the medical examination required to join the ESA. In fact, since she is 5.4 feet high, she is just above the established minimum height standard. Five years later, on November 30, 2014, she took off toward the International Space Station, greeting Earth with the same calm and confidence as someone sitting in a living room. During those two hundred days in space, she constantly kept in touch with the world through social media, giving interviews, and tweeting highly popular photos and updates.

She became immensely popular not just because of her courage and professional expertise, but also thanks to her joyful resourcefulness always accompanied by absolute discretion. "I'm not and I don't want to be a celebrity. Astronauts are not celebrities; we only communicate what we do and the experience we are lucky enough to live." Her next adventure was motherhood. It was never a limitation for her because she has always managed to balance family and professional life. "When there are two parents, the management of their children is not the sole responsibility of one of them but rather of the couple as a whole, and if it happens that one of them is very busy for a couple of years, then it's normal for the other to devote himself more to looking after the family." Samantha has now received the commission to go back into space as commander of Expedition 68, a responsibility that has never been assigned to a European woman before. "At ESA we encourage female participation because we want to prevent girls out there who might be perfect for the role from holding themselves back for fear of not being good enough." Samantha wants to encourage young aspiring lady astronauts to follow the path of their dreams, which is the most difficult and exciting path that may exist.

I CAN'T SEE ANY DIFFERENCE BETWEEN MEN AND WOMEN. THE ONLY DIFFERENCE IS BETWEEN THOSE WHO ARE COMPETENT AND THOSE WHO ARE NOT.

ELIZABETH DILLER

Behind the MoMA and the High Line, there is a rebel soul that calls into question the traditional concept of city by transforming the environment with striking projects, with the conviction that turning architecture into an experience is the winning idea.

When Elizabeth Diller graduated from the Cooper Union in Manhattan, she had no intention of designing homes and offices. "I never thought I was going to be an architect in the conventional sense," she admitted. Born in Poland and raised in New York, she chose to study architecture driven by an interest in art and the infinite potential of using urban space to create artistic experiences. She preserved this philosophy even after founding her own architecture studio together with Ricardo Scofidio, her professor who then also became her husband.

IF I HAD TO DESCRIBE MYSELF, I WOULD SAY THAT I AM AN ARTIST AND AN ARCHITECT WITHOUT MENTIONING BEING A WOMAN.

For twenty years, they did not design any buildings and devoted themselves to university teaching and art installations that sent intellectual elites into rapture but scared potential clients. "It took decades to start working as architects. Ricardo and I have always taught at the university to support ourselves." Then things changed. They were the first architects to receive the much-coveted MacArthur fellowship in 1999. Meanwhile, they rose to international prominence thanks to the impressive projects designed by the Diller Scofidio + Renfro studio. Elizabeth realized public spaces that have made the history of architecture, such as the New York High Line, an abandoned elevated freight rail line turned into a pedestrian area, and the Zaryadye Park in Moscow, just a few steps from Red Square, but also the futuristic Broad Museum in Los Angeles and two symbols of Manhattan, the new wing of the MoMA and the Shed, a flexible art space for performances and concerts. For her, the challenge has always been to imagine the future of new buildings, designing them in accordance with the idea of the city as a public asset. "In a rapidly changing world we build fixed, expensive, and permanent giants.

Building new ones without imagining a new paradigm that will make sense even in forty years makes our work obsolete even before it is concluded." The only architect who appeared twice in the *Time*'s list of the 100 most influential people, Elizabeth claims she has benefited from the strength of the feminist movement. "I never had any doubt that everything was accessible to me. Having said that, it is right to maintain the alert level on gender issues. Because if academic architecture has no prejudices, architecture as a profession is full of them. The image of the hero architect is still that of the white and visionary male. And if half of the students are women, only 20 percent actually work because the opportunities are lacking especially for them." She is committed to doing her part. In addition to running a studio that is sensitive to employees wanting to start and raise a family, she is aware of the importance of setting a good example. Equal pay and opportunities are fundamental rights, according to the winner of the 2019 Jane Drew Prize, which Elizabeth won "for raising the profile of women in architecture."

BILLIE EILISH

The voice of Generation Z has redefined the rules of the game like no other in music. Passing from a baggy to a pin-up style, Billie Eilish defeated any form of body shaming with her magic formula: "I am the only person I have to like."

Posting a photo on social media and getting a million likes in six minutes is possible if your name is Billie Eilish and you appear on the cover of *Vogue* with a look that radically revolutionizes your image. Blond, with a hairstyle reminiscent of a 1950s pin-up, this femme fatale version of the artist until now known for her baggy and genderless style (as well as for the iconic neon green strands of hair) was so disruptive, and not just for an aesthetic reason. The empowerment message that she conveyed shook things up in the fashion and communication worlds. "Suddenly you're a hypocrite if you want to show your skin, and you're easy. Well, if I am, then I'm proud. Me and all the girls are."

WHAT'S THE POINT OF **PLEASING** OTHER **PEOPLE?** YOU'VE GOT TO GET OUT AND **CHANGE** THE WORLD, AND WE'RE THE **GENERATION** THAT'S GOING TO STEP INTO THAT.

"Let's turn this concept around and be empowered by that. Showing your body should not take any respect away from you," said Billie in a powerful interview with *Vogue* where she spared no one: men, power dynamics, social media, fashion expectations, and patriarchal standards of beauty. "If you want to get surgery, go get surgery. If you want to wear a dress that somebody thinks that you look too big wearing, do it, if you feel like you look good, you look good." This message had a great impact on a generation that is still searching for its own identity. After all, the twenty-year-old Billie Eilish is still evolving, and she is perfectly aware of that: "You're not even supposed to really know who you are until you're at least my age." By playing with her image, the singer with 45 million monthly listeners on Spotify loudly asserts her desire for a rebirth, both for herself and for all the girls who choose her as a role model. While talking about the eating disorders from which she suffered as a young girl, she said that the rejection of her own body was the initial reason for her depression, from which she recovered thanks to her refound ability to feel good about herself.

Billie grew up singing in the Los Angeles Children's Chorus, and she achieved an unexpected success when she debuted online with her first single *Ocean Eyes*, which brought her to the top of the charts when she was only thirteen. With this first success, she did not only create music, but also a style that represented something new that never existed before, a mix of gender-fluid inspiration with clothes from the world of skaters and hip-hop that made her body inscrutable. The new version of Billie shocked some of her fans who wanted her to remain suspended—like Peter Pan—in the exact state in which they first encountered her. "People hold on to these memories, but it's very dehumanizing," she commented.

Yesterday as today, she goes her own way, without being influenced by the fashions of the moment. "I am who I am. I am the only person I have to like," said the seven-time Grammy winner, raising the stakes with her new album, *Happier Than Ever*. An ideal manifesto for a young woman who is increasingly aware of her uniqueness.

THERE ARE STILL PEOPLE WHO ARE AFRAID OF SUCCESSFUL WOMEN, AND THAT'S SO LAME.

ALICE FARNHAM

Talent, expertise, perseverance, but also authority: this is what it takes to conduct an orchestra, both for men and women, without distinction. By waving her baton, Alice encourages young women musicians to go on stage and fly higher and higher with the wings of music.

The podium requires backbone, but also the courage to face a double judgment because there is an audience behind your back and in front of you there are masters of the orchestra that you have to conduct. That is why holding a baton has much to do with leadership, to which men reluctantly renounce. "It is still unusual to see female conductors. Until the representation changes, girls tend not to see themselves in that role," claims Alice. Not even she imagined it when, at the age of eighteen, she found herself with a baton in her hand conducting a choir. "My first experience of conducting was mortifying—I was so nervous and had no idea how I was going to tell people what to do. It was the last profession I imagined entering."

THIS IDEA THAT IT HAS TO BE A MAN ON THE PODIUM HAS BEEN SO INGRAINED THAT WOMEN JUST COULDN'T SEE THEMSELVES IN THAT POSITION. I THOUGHT: LET'S CHANGE THAT.

At that time, she was studying music at Oxford, and she did not have ambitions of conducting, but over time, she found she liked that role. "It took me two or three embarrassing years trying to conduct the chapel choir and college music society before I suddenly realized I loved it." Little by little, she learned to manage tension, and by the time she graduated she had already discovered her vocation. In order to improve herself, she decided to move to Russia with the idea of staying just for three months to study with the renowned orchestra conductor Ilya Musin in Saint Petersburg. She ended up staying there for three years, never looking back. "If I had known then how hard it would be, I sometimes think, would I have really done that?" As soon as she returned to the UK, she achieved her first successes, and she realized that conducting an orchestra is a profession for musicians, no matter if they're men or women. According to Alice, anyone who studied music, can play an instrument, and has enough charisma can enter this profession. So, she decided to support and encourage young women musicians to choose a career like hers by holding the Women Conductors seminars. Over the years, she obtained the cooperation of great orchestras: the Royal Opera House, the English National Ballet, and the BBC Concert Orchestra. "I don't want to force anyone to conduct, and it's certainly not for everyone. But I want to inspire young women and show them that conducting is an option—something that they may not have even considered before—and these courses offer a safe place to have a go." As artistic director of the Royal Philharmonic Society's project, Alice has worked with more than five hundred female musicians, giving all of them the opportunity to hold a baton. "My main focus is to give them the confidence to stand in front of people and be a bigger version of themselves." But her ambition is far greater, and it is that one day as many women will conduct orchestras as men. "I think we've got a way to go. Until then, I will be championing these women and making sure their careers blossom."

TATYANA FAZLALIZADEH

Her canvas is the street, and the posters she draws are available to anyone who wants to share her fight against harassment because women's smiles depend first and foremost on respect.

"My name is not baby." "Stop telling women to smile." "Women are not outside for your entertainment." These are the kinds of warnings that you can find on the walls of half the world, from Philadelphia to Paris, accompanied by hand-drawn portraits of women and affixed on the walls as if they were advertisements or election posters. But there is no marketing strategy behind it. There is only the anger and frustration of an artist who is also a woman and as such becomes the target of unpleasant approaches that still too many men allow themselves to have when they see a woman walking by. "I wanted to talk about street harassment, so it made the most sense for me to do the work in the street."

I WANT TO MAKE WORK FOR OUR SOCIETY, TO MOVE IT TO BE A BETTER PLACE.

"The street is a different canvas, a different place to put your work on. I use the environment as part of the art," explained Tatyana while talking about *Stop Telling Women to Smile*, her most famous project, which also became a book. "The project was born for this. To make it clear that women should be free to take the train, go shopping, or go to school without having to change their route to avoid men who try to approach them as soon as they see them. It is not okay to stop and hold them to force them to speak, it is not okay to ask them to smile. This does not mean that the interaction between men and women on the street should be zero. It just means that everything should happen in a safe and respectful way." Tatyana started affixing her posters in 2012, spreading a message that over the years went far beyond the American borders. "The work has been installed on the walls in cities I've never been to," explained Tatyana, who has given everyone the chance to download her posters from the website www.stoptellingwomentosmile.com so as to affix them in their own neighborhoods.

Born and raised in Oklahoma, she studied art in Philadelphia, and right there, while she was working on a mural, she heard some men making unpleasant comments behind her, thus inspiring her project that then grew thanks to the accounts of other women. Tatyana made a portrait of each of those women with a message directed to men. Her project had a wide media echo that brought her to the pages of the *New York Times* and even captured the attention of Spike Lee, who took inspiration from her to write the TV series *She's Gotta Have It*. The director asked for her collaboration not only in realizing the works that appear in the series, but also as adviser in the creation of the main character, Nora Darling, a young artist who creates the series of posters *My Name Isn't*. Creative and tireless, Tatyana addressed, with the same audacity, the delicate issue of abortion and the shadow of racism. She made her feelings public with *America Is Black,* a mural showing a series of portraits of women including her mother, accompanied by these lines: "America is Black. It is native. It wears a hijab. It is a Spanish-speaking tongue. It is migrant. It is a woman. It is here. Has been here. And it's not going anywhere."

IT'S ART, IT DOESN'T HAVE TO BE PERFECT. IT'S SUPPOSED TO CHANGE, IT'S SUPPOSED TO EVOLVE.

CHIARA FERRAGNI

The world's number one fashion influencer is an Italian digital entrepreneur who addresses her fans with spontaneity and honesty. She built an empire starting from a blog. Her secret? Self-confidence.

Before the millions of followers, the covers, and the contracts worth millions of dollars, she was an ordinary young girl, but she had something special: a dream and the determination to fulfill it, as well as a family that has always believed in her. "I gained most of my self-confidence during my childhood, thanks to my mother, who used to tell me and my sisters: whatever you want, you will be able to do it. Ever since we were little, she encouraged us not to look for Prince Charming, but to be independent"—a lesson she learned perfectly, and that she personalized with a touch of sweetness.

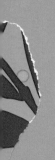

become a model of success that is even studied at the Harvard Business School. Her unstoppable ascent counts 26 million followers on Instagram, countless contracts with the most powerful international brands, a fortune worth millions of dollars, and a new family, which has expanded with the arrival of two children, Leone and Vittoria. Many people still look down on her, but in order to build an empire like hers, it takes more than a benevolent fate. In a period when social media plays a pivotal role, Chiara fully understands the responsibility she has toward her followers. "Using your influence to promote a product or collaborate with a brand is very nice, but I think it's important to use this influence also to share values and take a stand: it's time for social responsibility, it's time to be a little less impartial and to fight for the causes you believe in." She follows this same principle also when she fights for gender equality. "Women are at the heart of my world. They are the majority both in my work team and my family. But it takes more than a single day to make a revolution and my goal is to fight more and more battles to express the values I believe in, fighting for them personally."

ODILE GAUTREAU

With her atypical beauty and strong personality, this model is not only the face, but also the voice of all women who choose to be free to show themselves to the world as they are, without any label or filter.

She proudly flaunts her freckles scattered on her face like a constellation, her unmistakable red hair enhanced by an afro hairstyle, and the soft curves of her body. A successful model, Odile is the symbol of the body positive movement that breaks all stereotypes and encourages women to show themselves with pride, regardless of their body shape, age, skin color, or disabilities. "It's learning to be benevolent with your body, to cherish it, and above all to do the same with that of others," she sums up. On her Instagram account @ogqueen, she shows with no filters a physique that, according to the standards imposed by society, is not "normal" for a top model. Hers is not a provocation, but a stance: "This way we get used to the beauty of the difference and the expression of all women's bodies."

THERE ARE NO **RULES**, WE **HAVE** TO **FORGET DIKTATS** AND NOT TO SEEK AN **INSANE PERFECTION** ANYMORE.

In contrast with the invasion of white and ultrathin models parading on the catwalk, Odile beautifully stands out with her beauty still little celebrated because it's considered atypical, a word she hates. "Our relationship with the world is largely determined by the images we absorb. I play at changing the codes," she tells magazines, on which she appears more and more often thanks to the slow but inexorable revolution that is changing the rules of the fashion world, which is finally including less standardized bodies and different complexions. She uses her voice to help women to love themselves and their physical appearance by talking about her story and the toilsome self-acceptance journey she embarked on. Today, she is a committed model, but her fight started long ago. The daughter of an Ivorian mother and a French father, as a child she used to leaf through women's magazines, and she noticed that most women looked nothing like her. She was always mocked by her schoolmates for her frizzy hair and so she used to try to straighten it so as not to feel different from the other girls.

As a teenager, she decided to start an obstacle course that would lead her to the acceptance of her body. Encouraged by her friends, she sent her photos to *Paulette* magazine, where the protagonists are the readers themselves. In the blink of an eye, she was on the cover. After having walked the catwalk during the Fashion Weeks of half the world and posing for campaigns of brands like Nike and L'Oréal, she stood out also on magazines by relying precisely on her unconventionality and the messages she wants to convey. This choice allows her to share those models of inclusion that inspire her choices, like the icon of the struggle for civil rights Angela Davis. "Her fights against racism and sexism helped me build my own identity." Proud and aware of her uniqueness, Odile embodies a new femininity that is able to overturn the traditional canons of beauty. "Each woman blooms and grows her own way; this is what makes us all unique."

I REALIZED I HAD ALWAYS LOVED AND ACCEPTED MYSELF, BUT IT WAS THE OTHERS WHO MADE ME NOT LOVE MYSELF.

FABIOLA GIANOTTI

The first woman to be Director-General of CERN, Fabiola leads a community of 17,000 scientists with 110 different nationalities. She is an icon of progress and cooperation, because in the world's largest laboratory, the passion for science has neither gender nor passport.

When CERN was inaugurated on September 29, 1954, in the midst of the Cold War, she was not even born yet. Today, she directs it, advancing the idea that CERN is first and foremost a laboratory producing peace. In this magical place in Geneva, where particles are accelerated and the mysteries of the universe explored, researchers coming from nations at war with each other work side by side, and Nobel Prize winners cooperate with young students on a daily basis. They all have in common a passion for science and knowledge that nourishes a spirit of international cooperation. Since 2016, CERN has for the first time been directed by a woman, Fabiola Gianotti, who, given the renewed confidence, will hold this position until 2025.

GIRLS, CONTINUE THE PATH OF SCIENCE WITH COURAGE. IT IS NOT A WORLD FOR MEN ONLY.

"It is a great honor and privilege, but also a huge responsibility," she said, anticipating her objectives for the future, like the construction of Science Gateway, a building designed by Renzo Piano that will bring children closer to the mysteries of physics, and many other projects involving all continents. "We organize physics training activities in Africa, producing a snowball effect because every time you manage to sow a seed of knowledge, it reproduces and spreads," she explained. Fabiola's other priority is to increasingly involve women in a research field that has been considered "masculine" for far too long. "We are still far from numerical parity, but when I came here in 1994, we were less than 10 percent and now we reached 20 percent, so there has been a great progress. It is false to say that science is not for women: there are no women's or men's jobs. Science is for everyone," claims Fabiola. And there is no one better than her to prove it. Immediately after graduating with a physics degree (and also after a diploma in piano from the Conservatory), she was immediately ready to leave for Meyrin, in the Canton of Geneva on the border

YOU CAN'T MEASURE SUCCESS IF YOU HAVE NEVER FAILED.

Without ever losing her natural elegance, the following year she defeated all her opponents, and she managed to win the Golden Slam, a single achievement that includes all four Grand Slam titles and the Olympic gold medal. She became the number one player in the world, a position she held for 377 weeks, thanks to her iron character and her athletic, agile, and strong physique. The press said that she had the nicest legs on the tennis courts. In 1989, there was a sense that she was going to win the Grand Slam again, but it vanished when she lost in the final of the French Open, against the implacable Spanish Arantxa Sánchez, who broke up her rhythm. It was a startling revelation, as if everyone abruptly realized that Steffi could be defeated. The wheel has come full circle on that same tennis court in the center of Paris. Steffi loved the French Open tournament with all her heart, and her love was returned. So much so that she was exceptionally allowed to take home with her the door of her locker, number 19. Today, in its place there is the number 18B. Back then, she was only thirty, but she had already achieved everything she wanted in tennis. "I feel I have nothing left to accomplish," she said. After winning twenty-two Grand Slam tournaments and any other prize that matters, she decided to quit, but in her own way. With the same effort she put into tennis, the shy Steffi, who used to hide behind her trophies, is committed to staying out of the spotlight, with no biographies worth millions of dollars, very few interviews, and zero high society. She made only a few public appearances as ambassador of the Children for Tomorrow foundation, which she established in 1998 to help children born in war zones. No one knew she had secretly started dating Andre Agassi. As soon as they got married, the couple immediately received great acclaim. These two beloved champions make a perfect couple, made of two people who spent most of their lives with a tennis racket in their hands, always respecting each other. Just as in an endless tennis match where the ball always goes back on the other side.

NEVER LOOK BACK, I LOOK FORWARD.

KIRSTEN GREEN

She is a regular on the list of the most powerful women compiled by Forbes *every year. Trusting her intuition, she funds women-run startups, and she supports women entrepreneurs, by hunting for "unicorns."*

She is one of the one hundred most influential people according to *Time*. She has been named one of the twenty top venture capitalists by the *New York Times* and she was included more than once in *Forbes'* Midas List. She won the TechCrunch's Crunchies Awards and has been included in *Vanity Fair*'s New Establishment list. "Silicon Valley needs more venture capitalists like Kirsten, who not only hires women, but also seeks out women-led businesses to invest in," *Time* wrote. By hunting for "unicorns," as they are called in financial jargon, she invested in private companies that managed to achieve a market valuation of more than a billion dollars.

WE NEED TO HAVE MORE WOMEN FOUNDERS STEPPING UP TO KIND OF OWN THEIR OWN STORY AND ASK FOR WHAT THEY WANT.

And it is even better for her if there is a woman leading those companies, given that Kirsten invests almost half of her capital in women-run businesses, even if she plays it down: "We never invest in a male, we never invest in a female, we just invest in the right entrepreneur." People like her, who are able to achieve success thanks to their ideas, following uncertain and unconventional paths. Kirsten never attended a business school and never worked in a venture capital business before founding her own. However, she did spend more than a decade as a retail analyst, thus enjoying a privileged observation point that allowed her to study the retail landscape and its evolution closely. Originally from Moraga, California, Kirsten worked as an accountant and analyst before taking the plunge and starting her own business. In 2010 she founded Forerunner Ventures, choosing to venture into a definitely sexist environment where women still represent a minority. "There's really no good excuse for that kind of disparity," Kirsten says.

That's why she works behind the scenes to try to grant equal opportunities of success for businesswomen in the world of investment and technology. With the help of other managers like her, she created All Raise, a tutoring project supporting female entrepreneurship. The aim is to double the percentage of women entrepreneurs over the next ten years and increase funding for their projects. "We're with companies that are trying to reshape society, so it's almost more important than anywhere else that we have a good picture of diversity. I was really fortunate that our group collectively was more motivated about change than they were about complaining, and so we kind of just got together and thought, what can we do about it?" Thanks to her visibility, Kirsten can take a public stand against sexism, committing herself to enabling women to realize what she managed to do. "People need role models, and they need to feel that there's this opportunity to learn. They need to have people that will stick up for them. I want to be a part of that."

THERE'S NOT ENOUGH OF US AND WE'VE GOT TO CHANGE THINGS.

MARISA HAMAMOTO

With her performances, she breaks down all stereotypes about dance. So much so that she created a dance company open to dancers with or without disabilities to promote inclusion, because dancing is a right with no barriers.

Marisa is a survivor. She was sexually assaulted, suffered discrimination, and experienced racism, but most of all, she had a stroke that left her paralyzed from the neck down, thus putting her dream of becoming a dancer on hold. Doctors warned her that she would probably never walk again, but she did not give up and after two months she was already back on her feet. However, her scars were much deeper since they were provoked by post-traumatic stress disorder caused by body shaming and a form of racism related to her origins (her father is from Honolulu and her mother is Japanese), which emerged during the years she spent in the United States and Japan, where she always felt out of place.

INSTEAD OF THINKING SOMETHING DOESN'T WORK, WE THINK, "HOW CAN THIS WORK?"

"I was still paralyzed on the inside," she said while explaining her decision to quit the dance world for almost four years. During that really hard time, she found out that she was not alone. "One in five people have a disability, which means a billion people, and yet the world is neither accessible nor inclusive. When you are set aside, you stop feeling human." Everything changed when she met Adelfo Cerame Jr., a paraplegic athlete. "I realized that dancing with Adelfo was nothing different from anyone else. Dance is a universal language. Dance doesn't discriminate." As soon as she realized that there were very few dance schools offering an opportunity to people in wheelchairs, Marisa decided to fix this. In 2015, she founded Infinite Flow, a nonprofit company headquartered in Los Angeles that includes dancers with and without disabilities. The goal is clear: to break down stereotypes and promote inclusion by welcoming people with all sorts of disabilities, including hearing, visual, and intellectual impairments. Since then, her online performances have been viewed by 75 million people and her dancers have participated in more than one hundred events, performing before audiences that have included students, executives of companies such as Apple, Facebook, and Porsche, and even people from the International Monetary Fund. Nevertheless, she felt the strongest emotions while performing for children in schools. "What you're exposed to as a child stays with you your whole life. So, when you're exposed to inclusion at a young age, it stays with you. I've seen the impact we have on children, and it's encouraged us to expand our youth program." Through the visibility she gains with her work, Marisa hopes she will inspire those who have suffered her same traumatic experiences, "women who look like me, who can learn it's possible to align your passions with your purpose and create a career out of it."

SHAMSIA HASSANI

Spray paint and brushes are the weapons of this street artist who paints the gentle strength of women on Kabul's walls. With their eyes closed and no lips, her indigo heroines ask to have a voice to be able to continue to pursue their dreams.

With her face wrapped in the traditional chador, a mask on her mouth and spray paint in her hand, Shamsia started a revolution in the streets of Kabul. The first street artist in Afghanistan chose to give a voice to women, bringing them outside the walls of their homes. "I want my art to live with people and become part of their daily lives," she told the *Guardian*. With her works, she is committed to building a female consciousness in a patriarchal society. The open-air gallery painted by Shamsia represents her way to fight Afghan women's isolation. "I want to show my art to those who have no access to visit galleries and exhibitions. Since women have more restrictions than men in our society, I chose my character to be a woman."

ART CHANGES PEOPLE'S MINDS AND PEOPLE CHANGE THE WORLD.

Born in Iran, Shamsia decided, in 2005, to move back to Kandahar, her parents' homeland, to study painting and visual arts at the University of Kabul, where she became one of the youngest professors. In 2010, she took her spray cans of a thousand shades of blue and she started making her graffiti on the walls of Afghan cities, which had remained silent until then. She made those walls the home of her indigo girls who look proud and sweet at the same time. Pensive, with downcast eyes and no lips, they are kind souls surrounded by rubble and terror, the expression of a voiceless world. Shamsia fortuitously paints them in a few minutes for fear of being discovered and punished. Indeed, making graffiti on the streets had always been a dangerous activity for a woman, even before the return of the Taliban, not only due to possible terrorist attacks, but also because most people do not appreciate this kind of art and believe it is not a good thing to do, especially for girls. "Only if the situation permits, maybe once every six months, I paint a very public space. Usually, I paint on destroyed walls with no owner."

Proud of her work, in all the pictures of her, Shamsia appears with a spray can in her hand intent on covering walls with colors while some look at her with curiosity and many others with suspicion. "I want to show that women have returned to Afghan society with a new, stronger shape. It's not the woman who stays at home. It's a new woman. A woman who is full of energy, who wants to start again. I want to say that people look at them differently now," she said in an interview with the magazine *ArtRadar,* published in 2014. Since Afghanistan plunged back into the darkness of the Taliban hell, she had to suspend her battle, but people rave about her works on social media. Many users from all over the world share her works on Instagram, Twitter, and Facebook. Meanwhile, Shamsia took refuge elsewhere, always finding exhibition spaces everywhere from Los Angeles to New York, Germany, Norway, and Italy. Wrapped in a long, deep blue chador, her girls continue to exist surrounded by flowers, butterflies, shells, or hugging a musical instrument because, as Shamsia says, "music, like art, sets us free." Surrounded by dancing notes that they emanate while playing their music, her girls have the strength to break the wall of violence with the power of lightness and the tenacity of their smile.

I WANT TO MAKE AFGHANISTAN FAMOUS BECAUSE OF ITS ART, NOT ITS WAR.

ARIANNA HUFFINGTON

She has always chased success, and failures never scared her. The historic foundress of the Huffington Post *managed to achieve all she ever dreamed of since her childhood: the most popular blog in the world, two daughters, and an address book with thousands of contacts.*

Hers is one of those stories that wows whoever deals with communication and journalism. How can one go from being a solitary teenager from Athens to becoming one of the most influential women of American journalism? With determination, courage, but most of all without ever letting your failures defeat you, just as she did. Born in Greece, Arianna Stassinopoulos comes from a traditional family that just hoped she could have a good match, but her ambitions were very different. She went to great lengths to win a scholarship and she managed to fly to Cambridge, one of the most prestigious universities in the world. It was her first victory over her family and thousands of other candidates.

these voices to participate in online debates. The first bloggers she invited to write were the well-known Arthur Schlesinger, the television writer Larry David, and the actor John Cusack. In 2006, Arianna was included among *Time*'s list of the one hundred most influential people in the world, and she was again in 2011. Her website managed to win the prestigious Pulitzer Prize before being sold to AOL for $315 million. At the age of sixty-six, she surprised everyone by deciding to move on and take on a new challenge with Thrive Global, a digital platform created to re-establish the importance of well-being over money and career. "I've always dreamed of making the way we live and work better. A nervous breakdown cannot be the price of success. That's what I want to achieve with my new company." This was the umpteenth challenge for this woman who, before achieving success, suffered more than one defeat, both in her personal and professional life. However, for her a failure is nothing more than a glitch. "Failure is not the opposite of success, it's part of success. In life, failure is inevitable. And the best leaders learn from their failure. They use it as a tool to become successful."

FATOUMATA KÉBÉ

As a little girl, she used to stay up at night to stargaze, and she then made a career out of it. Today she is among the brightest astrophysicists in Europe. What is her mission? To clean up space, and to convince all girls to conquer the sky.

She has always chased the moon since she began leafing through her father's astronomy encyclopedia when she was eight years old. And so, she became a brilliant astrophysicist constantly climbing the ranking of the most influential scientists in the world. French but with Malian origins, Fatoumata fulfilled her dream by studying fluid mechanics at the Pierre and Marie Curie University, and she then attended courses at the European Space Agency and at the French National Center for Scientific Research in Tokyo. "People are still surprised when I introduce myself as an astronomer."

at a very young ag[...] what men told me to do, I decided today I wanted to take the power ba[...] wear pants." With the same sincerity, she spoke about how her classma[...] ully her. "Some bullies used to take me and throw me into the trash b[...] to say that it's where I belonged, because I was trash," she told the *G*[...] ecalling the time when she ended up in the trash and she lost her j[...] ring she managed to overcome thanks to therapy and the creation [...] Way Foundation, through which she helps victims of bullying, di[...] sexual abuse. She has always used her voice not only to make h[...] dance all over the world, but also to support the causes she cares [...] TQ+ community rights. "You must be protected at all costs, like all [...] n Earth, and I will continue to write music for you and fight for you[...] ou not love her?

EVEN WHEN I TOUCH THE **BOTTOM**, THERE IS STILL A **PART** OF ME THAT WANTS TO **DANCE** AND **REJOICE**.

CHRISTINE LAGARDE

She is one of the very few women in the global governance stratosphere. A silver-haired iron lady, the president of the European Central Bank teaches the world her female empowerment lesson.

With her cool head, firm hand, and a woman's touch, Christine Lagarde is redefining the most powerful job of global finance. The president of the European Central Bank does a "man's job," as she herself demonstrated when she posted a photo on Twitter showing the executive board where she was installed in 2019. It was a round table with twenty-three men and one woman, herself. She sent a strong message that showed the world that equality remains a distant goal. She has never been prone to power games, and she rose to power without having to pass through the narrow corridors of politics.

I HAVE THE **TALENTS** OF **WOMEN: I AM PATIENT** AND **INCLUSIVE.**

She simply established herself, just as she did early in her career, when she worked at the American law firm Baker McKenzie, where she rose through the ranks until reaching the pinnacle. A model daughter of a Latin teacher and an English professor, Christine has come a long way since she used to look after her three little brothers in Le Havre, Normandy. Since then, she has always wanted to be at the top, and she started with becoming a synchronized swimming champion. This discipline taught her the first rule to follow: grit your teeth and smile. She did it also when she failed to pass the entrance exam to the ENA, the French National School of Administration, hotbed of the ruling class. She failed twice: the first time because, as she said, she was distracted by love. She was not discouraged, and she started achieving one record after another. She was the first woman to be appointed Minister of the Economy and Finance in France, and the first female Managing Director of the International Monetary Fund. Is it determination? Definitely, but not exclusively. Her empowerment lesson comes from the heart, because, according to Christine, to reach the top you mainly need self-esteem, which arises from the affection of those close to you.

"I don't wake up in the morning thinking, 'I am a role model,' but I am struck every time I am stopped by women of all ages and nationalities who tell me: you embody something that one day I could become, or something that one day my children could realize." She taught her two sons to be self-sufficient and not to depend on a wife who looks after them. "Mothers should teach their children to love and respect women. After all, men are the sons of their mothers." She currently fights to get the world to recognize feminine authority, and she still remembers when some clients of the law firm of which she was chairman used to ask her to serve some coffee because they believed she was the boss's secretary. After the outbreak of the Great Recession, she said that it would never have happened if Lehman Brothers bank had been called "Lehman Sisters." She is convinced that "giving more space to women in organizations leads to improved governance mechanisms and better decision-making capacity." After all, she is surely a very straightforward person, and, when asked if in her career less-qualified men had ever passed her by, she replied with a smile, "Sure, but they didn't last long."

I THINK THAT WOMEN ARE RESILIENT, AS MANY STUDIES SHOW. AND RESILIENCE IN THE FACE OF CHANGE IS SOMETHING WE BADLY NEED.

ANNIE LEIBOVITZ

All her life she has been chasing pictures. All the celebrities from the world of show business, sports, and politics were captured by her camera. Nevertheless, she does not consider herself a photographer, but "a conceptual artist using photography."

Who can persuade the Queen of England to take her crown off for an official portrait? And who can bring together a hundred Hollywood stars for a group shot? The answer is Annie Leibovitz, the most known, sought-after, and highest-paid photographer in the world. She is responsible for pictures that became pieces of history, like the one portraying Yoko Ono and a naked John Lennon hugging each other a few hours before his murder; the picture of Patti Smith that appeared on the cover of the album *Gone Again*; of Whoopi Goldberg lying in a bathtub full of milk; of the *Star Wars* cast; of the rotundities of a pregnant Demi Moore, and also of Keith Haring's body in black and white.

I'VE NEVER LIKED THE WORD "CELEBRITY." I LIKE TO PHOTOGRAPH PEOPLE WHO ARE GOOD AT WHAT THEY DO.

She is also the photographer of Ground Zero's smoking ruins and of two editions of the iconic Pirelli Calendar. Hectic and a workaholic, she has a reputation for being tough. After all, rigor and authority are necessary to get what she wants. "I'm not good at putting the subjects I portray at ease. I am interested in their stories; I am a journalist. This is why my captions are just as important as the shots." Tall and always dressed in black, she never puts makeup on, and she moves surrounded by an army of assistants who help her compose impressive sceneries designed as film productions. She uses artifice to find naturalness and follow the bizarre intuitions that distinguish most of the pictures that made her famous. The third of six children, she grew up traveling from one military base to another with her father, an Air Force officer. "My first shot was the car window," she said while recalling the long journeys she made as a child in the backseat of the family station wagon, from Alaska to Texas, surrounded by the American landscape.

In 1970, after spending a year in a kibbutz in Israel, she started working for *Rolling Stone*, and she signed her first cover shortly afterward. She collected 142 of them by the end of this legendary partnership. Her working relationship with Susan Sontag, who would become her partner, was equally intense. Together they edited *Women*, a volume dedicated to the female figure with all its facets, with Annie's pictures and Susan's words, a work in progress that continued even after Susan's passing, with the aim of asserting feminine power and the role of women in contemporary society. Nudity appears in only a few shots, and never to display sensuality, but rather to emphasize the wonderful uniqueness of every woman and to move away from stereotypes and standards of beauty to which society has relegated women for far too long. "I don't even know how to define the idea of beauty, and maybe it's not even for an aesthetic reason. I guess I like to tell with my pictures who these women are and what they do."

PEOPLE BUY IDEAS, THEY DON'T BUY PHOTOGRAPHS.

SANNA MARIN

In a world where a woman leading a nation still makes the news, she is living proof that you should never be discouraged by stereotypes and sexist opinions. Self-determination, inclusion, and a desire for change guide her unstoppable ascent.

"I have never thought about my age or gender. I think of the reasons I got into politics, and those things for which we have won the trust of the electorate," she said as soon as she was elected Prime Minister of Finland at the age of only thirty-four. It was a necessary clarification, considering that Sanna embodied two of the characteristics traditionally most belittled and devalued by the most eminent personalities in the political world: being a woman and being young. With her all-female coalition, she proved she was able to rise to the challenge. A champion for the environment, she definitely made her voice heard at the Davos World Economic Forum with her powerful speeches on the most important global issues.

MY GENDER HAS ALWAYS BEEN THE STARTING POINT. I HOPE ONE DAY IT WON'T BE AN ISSUE.

"Finland is committed to being climate neutral by 2035—we see that climate change is the biggest risk humanity faces. But fighting climate change is a big opportunity for our technology, our businesses, creating new jobs, creating well-being." Her perspective helps to see things from a new point of view. Without half-measures, she clearly expressed her opinion on gender issues. "Everyone should have the right to determine their own identities," she told the BBC. "It's not my job to identify people. It's everyone's job to identify themselves. It's not my place to say." Hers are not empty words because Sanna knows what she talks about very well. She grew up in an LGBTQ+ family with two mothers, one of whom is her biological mother. As a child, she felt invisible because she was not able to speak openly about her situation. A working-class child, she was the first of her family to finish high school and university studies, which she paid herself by working as a store clerk. She started her political career from the bottom in Tampere, with the elections of the town council, and she then rose through the ranks until she entered

Parliament. On December 10, 2019, she was elected Prime Minister of Finland. What did she have to sacrifice to achieve all of this? Nothing, apparently. When she obtained the office, she had recently become a mother. Her daughter Emma was born only a year before, but Sanna was able to manage her role of mother thanks to a welfare system on which Finnish mothers can rely, thus proving that it is possible to reconcile family and professional life. Her femininity, too, has never been questioned. When she posed for a photo with a blazer and nothing underneath, many said it was not appropriate, but Finnish women defended Sanna with the hashtag #ImWithSanna, reminding everyone that the way a woman dresses is certainly not a good reason for belittling her skills. Included in *Time*'s 100 Next, the list of the one hundred emerging personalities who are shaping the future, she perfectly embodies a positive message, not only for her countrymen, but for the whole world. She is a leader capable of demonstrating with facts what "equal opportunities" really means.

RIGOBERTA MENCHÚ

Respect for the environment, protection of the Mayan culture, and the fight against any form of social and civil abuse are the pillars of the peace lesson taught by the Nobel Prize winner Rigoberta Menchú, who fights with her words, armed only with her brightly colored traditional dresses and her disarming smile.

Rigoberta was only thirty-three years old when she was awarded the Nobel Peace Prize in 1992 "in recognition of her work for social justice and ethno-cultural reconciliation based on respect for the rights of indigenous peoples." With her spirit and fortitude, she has been able to rebel against the desire for revenge by responding to abuses with forgiveness. She is a living testimony to how an atrocious fate can be turned into an exemplary story, by always staying true to the way of thinking that guides every action of this courageous woman: "Peace cannot exist without justice, justice cannot exist without fairness, fairness cannot exist without development, development cannot exist without democracy, democracy cannot exist without respect for the identity and worth of cultures and peoples."

I RESOLUTELY BELIEVE THAT RESPECT FOR DIVERSITY IS A FUNDAMENTAL PILLAR IN THE ERADICATION OF RACISM, XENOPHOBIA, AND INTOLERANCE.

Raised during the civil war that caused a bloodbath in Guatemala, she worked since childhood as a farmhand. She was only 16 when she had to flee, on foot, to seek refuge in Chiapas. She brutally lost most of her family: her father was burned alive, her mother killed, and her two brothers murdered. It is a terrible story that happened to them and to many other victims of these perpetrators who have now been charged with genocide against the Mayan people. Some people chose to respond with a guerrilla war, but she started a peaceful struggle by denouncing the Guatemalan regime and the systematic violation of human rights against the indigenous people. Bishop Samuel Ruiz invited that courageous teenager to tell her story to the Mexican Episcopal Conference. Rigoberta was illiterate, but she left everyone speechless by showing her natural charisma and a spiritual strength that marked the beginning of a long journey for her. That day, she discovered that her strength lies in her words.

With words and no weapons, she started fighting the dictatorship and she contributed to defeat it. Her commitment would lead her to defeat an army with just the power of her voice, by actively participating in the commission that in 1996 laboriously ended hostilities in Guatemala. "Anyone like me who has dedicated their life to fighting impunity and injustice has a duty to be optimistic. Today and forever. The past cannot be changed. We can, however, prevent it from happening again by building a more humane future for those who will come. This is our commitment as men and women and I'm convinced that it's worth it." After the Nobel Prize, she became a UN Messenger of Peace and she created the Rigoberta Menchú Tum Foundation, which promotes the defense of human rights, peace, and sustainable development. Time goes by, but the former farmhand from Chimel continues to fight for environmental protection, the dignity of Native Americans, education, and justice. "Peace is not the signing of a treaty. It is a daily choice. Everyone can make a difference."

ANGELA MERKEL

With the disarming simplicity of her language and habits, she has managed to succeed on the German and world stage, facing a man's world and sweeping away any gender stereotype for good.

In Germany, her name has even become a verb: "merkelize," which means to achieve the objective, but gradually. "Leisurely but tirelessly," Johann Wolfgang von Goethe would have told her if he had known her. The daughter of a Lutheran pastor and an English teacher, she was supposed to become a physics researcher in a university somewhere in East Germany, where her parents moved from the western part of the country. It was quite an exceptional situation at a time when German people would have done anything to go westward. A scientist brought into politics, and never garish, Angela relied on the "surprise effect" throughout her life.

YOU DO NOT RAISE A PROBLEM IF YOU DO NOT ALSO HAVE THE SOLUTION TO SOLVE IT.

Starting from the sidelines allows you more freedom of action, and Angela had guessed it since the very beginning. Thus, she never showed off to avoid scaring the others, especially men, who often made a huge mistake by underestimating her. Everyone fell for it, including Helmut Kohl, the Christian Democratic Union leader and icon of the struggle for a unified Germany, who kicked off her brilliant career by appointing her as Minister of Women and Youth. He thought she was harmless and maneuverable, and so he used to call her "Mädchen," meaning "the girl," or better, "my girl." Of course, Kohl was very much mistaken. When he realized it, it was too late, and Angela had already taken his place as head of the Chancery. No one spoke anymore of "Mädchen," because now everyone had to call her "die Kanzlerin." And they would have to call her that for the following sixteen years, until 2021. On a scale that measures the duration of the power democratically granted by popular vote, her four mandates are a figure close to eternity. So much so that, in Germany, there is a well-known story of a child asking her mother: "Mom, can a man become chancellor?" It seems a paradox, or maybe not, because there is an entire generation of German people who believe the head of government has always had the face of a woman: Angela Merkel.

Ten years after her election, she surprised everyone when she decided to open the doors to the thousands of migrants thronging on the borders, and she allowed many asylum-seekers who had applied for entering Europe to go to Germany. She thus proved once more that under her gentle and obliging appearance, she is made of the same steel used by the Krupps to manufacture cannons and locomotives for all Europe's empires. *Time* referred to her as "Chancellor of the free world" in 2015, when it named her person of the year with the following words: "Her leadership has helped preserve and promote an open, borderless Europe in the face of economic turmoil and an ongoing refugee crisis." Her departure from the scene is bound to split the history of German politics in two parts, one with her and the other without. She retired from politics at the height of her success, with a simple but solemn ceremony. Wrapped in a black coat and illuminated only by torches held by Bundeswehr soldiers, she gave her speech. A legacy made of elegance and political wisdom, which she ended with an encouragement to young people: "I would like to encourage you in the future to look at the world from other people's perspectives as well," just as she did, well aware of her role. A woman in a man's world.

THE QUESTION IS NOT WHETHER WE ARE ABLE TO CHANGE BUT WHETHER WE ARE CHANGING FAST ENOUGH.

NADIA MURAD

She rose like a phoenix from the destructive and violent trauma she suffered at the hands of ISIS terrorists. "I want to be the last girl in the world with a story like mine," she repeats whenever she can. That's why she travels around the world demanding justice on behalf of all Yazidi women.

When she was a child and she lived in the village of Kocho in northern Iraq, her dream was to open a beauty parlor. She did not know the Nobel Prize existed, and neither could she conceive the evil she would have to face. At the age of twenty-one, Nadia was kidnapped by ISIS, forced to convert to Islam, and sold repeatedly as a sex slave. Not only did she lose her mother and six brothers, but also the chance of leading a normal life. "My life as a simple Yazidi farm girl is gone forever, the dreams and hopes of my whole community are gone." After months of captivity, she managed to escape taking advantage of a door left unlocked by one of her captors. She then crossed Iraqi Kurdistan to reach a refugee camp and then Germany, where she sought refuge.

MY **STORY** IS THE BEST **WEAPON** I HAVE AGAINST **TERRORISM**, AND I PLAN ON **USING** IT UNTIL THOSE TERRORISTS ARE **PUT ON TRIAL.**

From there, she started shaping her new future, marked by a trauma that could have annihilated anyone but her. Thousands of other Yazidi women shared the same fate, but Nadia decided to show the world her wounds with a clear purpose: to become an advocate for her people as well as all victims of human trafficking and violence. "We are activists, and we need more than empathy," she said. Thanks to her courage, she was the first Iraqi person to receive, at the age of only twenty-five, the most prestigious humanitarian award: the Nobel Peace Prize. The words she said when she received the prize sound more like a wish than a speech: "I hope that today marks the beginning of a new era—when peace is the priority, and the world can collectively begin to define a new roadmap to protect women, children, and minorities from persecution, in particular victims of sexual violence." Today, she travels around the world to raise public awareness, a weighty task that shows the generous soul of a young girl whose dream of an ordinary life was wiped out by the violence she suffered.

I AM THE FORMER FIRST LADY OF THE UNITED STATES AND ALSO A DESCENDANT OF SLAVES. IT'S IMPORTANT TO KEEP THAT TRUTH RIGHT THERE.

At the age of four, she could read, and she forged ahead at school, too: she got her diploma when she was seventeen, and then, at the age of twenty-one, she graduated with honors in sociology from the illustrious Princeton University. Three years later, she obtained her Juris Doctor from Harvard. Prestigious results that, however, caused her suffering because during those years Michelle experienced how skin color still carries weight. In her dissertation, she wrote: "Regardless of the circumstances under which I interact with Whites at Princeton, it often seems as if, to them, I will always be Black first and a student second." She met her future husband at the law firm where she had already made a name for herself, while he was starting out as an intern. Michelle mentored him, and she ended up marrying him. Pragmatism, the power of persuasion, and efficiency have always been her strengths, also when, with the births of Malia and Sasha, she decided to reduce her work commitments to devote herself to her family, her true priority. In all her interviews, she always pointed out that she is "Mom first, political wife second." Beautiful and elegant (according to *Vanity Fair* one of the ten best-dressed women in the world), she has always been in the forefront of the fight for equal rights and gender equality. By taking advantage of the visibility of her role, Michelle managed, as First Lady, to

I DON'T REALLY KNOW WHAT FEELING JAPANESE OR HAITIAN OR AMERICAN IS SUPPOSED TO FEEL LIKE. I JUST FEEL LIKE ME.

At the age of twenty-two, *Forbes* mentioned her as the highest paid athlete of all time, *Sports Illustrated* named her Sportswoman of the Year, and *Time* included her among the world's one hundred most influential people for two consecutive years. With a tennis racket in her hand, she is relentless, and she challenged legendary champions. In her early twenties, Naomi was ready to follow in the footsteps of her idol, Serena Williams, whom she beat in 2018 thanks to her powerful serve and a forehand that won her four Grand Slam tournaments. However, what makes her unique are not only her sports skills, but rather her identity as a woman and a sportswoman characterized by contradictions, facets, and meeting points between cultures, passions, and missions. With her enthusiasm, but especially with her weaknesses, Naomi embodies the spirit of a new generation. Like when she said that "it's okay not to be okay.," explaining her decision to take a break because everyone, even champions, has their weak moments. To prove who she is, on and off the court, she supports the causes that most matter to her with the same determination with which she defeats her opponents.

"Talk about it, and never stop doing it" is the magic formula of her commitment, which she explains in a shy voice loaded with powerful content, just as Kobe Bryant taught her: "I just want to be the type of person that he thought I was going to be." Thus, in support of Black Lives Matter, she made her appearance at the 2020 US Open wearing a different face mask for each match she played (and won), each one with the name of one of seven victims of racist police violence: Breonna Taylor, Elijah McClain, Ahmaud Arbery, Trayvon Martin, Philando Castile, Tamir Rice, and George Floyd. "Just because it isn't happening to you doesn't mean it isn't happening at all," she explained.

Her passion for manga made her a symbol for young Asians, her victories turned her into an international star, but the real peak of her fame came when she appeared on the cover of *Vogue*, photographed by Annie Leibovitz. Soon after that, Barbie dedicated a doll to her, naming her as a representative of a cultural revolution. For Naomi, there is no limit to dreams, as she herself wrote in a tweet where she announced her collaboration with Mattel: "I hope that every child is reminded that they can be and do anything."

YOU JUST GOTTA KEEP GOING AND FIGHTING FOR EVERYTHING, AND ONE DAY YOU'LL GET WHERE YOU WANT.

MARINA PISKLAKOVA-PARKER

An activist against violence toward women in Russia, Marina studied aeronautical engineering in Moscow, then she decided to devote herself full-time to victims of violence. Her safe houses are an always-turned-on light in the darkness of brutality.

One morning, while taking her son to school, she realized that one of the other moms had her face bruised and swollen. "Why don't you just leave your husband?" Marina asked her. "And where would I go?" she answered. As a matter of fact, there existed no support whatsoever for women victims of violence in Russia in 1993. Marriage could become a trap for many wives who had to juggle job and motherhood responsibilities without being protected in any way against abusive partners on whom they depended for their home and financial stability. It is a phenomenon so deeply rooted in Russia that there is even a saying: "He beats you, that means he loves you."

144

IT TAKES THE WHOLE COMMUNITY TO ADVANCE THE LIVES OF WOMEN.

Marina gave that woman the opportunity to unburden herself with someone who did not judge her. "I didn't realize I had actually started counseling her," she recalls. Shortly thereafter, she decided to start a help line and to open the first safe house. "When I started the first domestic violence hotline, I was alone, answering calls four hours a day, every day, for six months. I was counseling people in person the other four hours. I couldn't say no; there were so many women." Within a year, she managed to form the first group of volunteers to assist victims by phone, then she started giving courses in other cities, and she created new counseling centers and safe houses. Meanwhile, Marina also started psychological assistance programs that also include legal assistance for domestic abuse victims, and she created training courses for lawyers to teach them how to handle cases of domestic abuse. Russian law, in the case of litigation in court, allows the defense to use the "instigation to violence" as an extenuating circumstance to obtain a reduced sentence. The victim is charged with incitement so that she feels responsible for her own abuse, and it is against her that the lawyer of the adverse party lashes out, accusing her in front of all present at the trial. "This is perhaps the cruelest form of psychological abuse. Regrettably, there are still many judges who will readily accept the notion that she was in some way responsible, and let the perpetrator avoid being held accountable for his actions," explains Marina. From then on, she has been stubbornly fighting for the recognition of a phenomenon that continues to be considered a private affair. With the pandemic, the situation has worsened. "We don't have an effective response system, so women in Russia are much more vulnerable to domestic violence than in other countries," she told Euronews. Today, Marina is the president of ANNA (Association No to Violence), which manages a network of crisis centers all over the former Soviet Union. Awarded the Human Rights Global Leadership Award, she launched an awareness-raising campaign to make cases of domestic violence public and inform women about their rights. "Although in the constitution on the paper, women are announced to be equal, the reality is there is still a long way to go."

AMAL RAMZI ALAMUDDIN

Civic engagement, flawless looks, and absolute discretion: this describes the famous Lebanese lawyer, from the law courts where she stands for human rights to her wedding with a Hollywood star.

She defended Yazidi women reduced to sex slaves by ISIS militiamen, and she has been adviser to the former Secretary-General of the United Nations Kofi Annan. She teaches at universities, and she met the Pope, Angela Merkel, and David Cameron. She is always impeccably dressed, without ever having an accessory out of place or a mismatched detail. Amal looks so perfect that she does not even seem real. Even her husband admitted: "I feel like an idiot talking to my own wife." Those are George Clooney's words, the husband she married in Venice with a fairytale wedding and the father of her twins. A private person, Amal is not on social media, and since she married one of the most powerful stars in Hollywood, she has given only a couple of interviews, without ever talking about her private life.

WE DON'T WANT TO LOSE AN ENTIRE GENERATION BECAUSE THEY HAD THE BAD LUCK OF BEING BORN IN THE WRONG PLACE AT THE WRONG TIME.

"There's a lot of my work that takes place behind closed doors, that is not even seen. I think that if there are more people who now understand what's happening about the Yazidis and ISIS, and if there can be some action that results from that, that can help those clients, then I think it's a really good thing to give that case the extra publicity that it may get," she said in an interview with the BBC. She lets her husband talk about their family life. After her maternity leave, Amal did not waste any time and she went right back to work. After all, commitment runs in her family. Her grandmother was the first woman to graduate from Beirut American University, the same university where her father used to teach. Her grandfather was a minister, and her mother a television reporter.

Born in Lebanon, Amal moved to London with her family at the age of two, to escape the war. She studied law at Oxford, and she specialized at the New York University School of Law. She then started working for the Sullivan & Cromwell law firm, where she worked as a criminal lawyer on the Enron case, the massive financial fraud that caused a 20,000-employee company to collapse.

Amal first arrived at the London Doughty Street Chambers law firm (whose owner is the icon of the struggle for human rights Geoffrey Robertson) to hold a seminar. She then decided to stay to defend personalities such as Julian Assange and Yulia Tymoshenko. In 2005 she joined the UN Commission, in charge of shedding light on the former Lebanese Prime Minister Rafiq Hariri's murder. It was the beginning of a high-profile career at the UN. She spoke about humanitarian causes many times, and she served as a member of several committees. She bluntly expressed her opinion about the #MeToo movement: "I think because of the brave women who have come forward to tell their stories, the future workplace will be safer for my daughter than it was for people of my generation. We're in a situation where a predator feels less safe and a professional woman feels safer, and that's where we need to be."

Wise and forward-looking, Amal gave students of Vanderbilt University this encouragement: "Be courageous. Challenge orthodoxy. Stand up for what you believe in. When you are in your rocking chair talking to your grandchildren many years from now, be sure you have a good story to tell."

COURAGE IS CONTAGIOUS. PEOPLE WHO HAVE HAD THE COURAGE TO CHANGE THEIR SOCIETIES INSPIRE EACH OTHER AND CREATE RIGHTS FOR FUTURE GENERATIONS.

MEGAN RAPINOE

One of the stars of the United States women's national soccer team, Megan made her life a great fight not only for her own rights but also for those of her community and the most vulnerable. She fights in her own way for women, homosexuals, and all outcasts.

The captain of the US women's soccer team at the 2019 World Cup is not only a soccer player, one of the strongest wingers in the world, skilled at dribbling and able to build a long-lasting career, but is also a fighter, and the most political among soccer players. Megan has always been on the front line in the fight against the gender pay gap in the sports world. She supports those sportswomen who ask to be treated equally to men, at least when they play for the national team. Her life is a mission, and she is not afraid of getting involved in person, both in soccer and in life. And so, in 2016, she did not hesitate to kneel during the national anthem, risking her career to express solidarity with Colin Kaepernick, the American football player who first protested in the name of racial issues with that same act.

BE MORE, BE BETTER, BE BIGGER THAN YOU'VE EVER BEEN BEFORE.

Criticisms came immediately but were soon overwhelmed by a giant groundswell of support. "Of course, it's a privilege for me to pull on the jersey. Part of that privilege is representing America, and representing America is representing all of America," she said while explaining her act. After studying sociology and political science at the University of Portland, Oregon, Megan started playing soccer in the Women's Premier Soccer League, and she then led the American national soccer team, winning the Ballon d'Or, two World Cups, and an Olympic Game.

A proud advocate of LGBTQ+ rights, she is homosexual, and she never hid it. She is in a relationship with Sue Bird, the point guard of the American national basketball team. The two combined have won five Olympic gold medals, and they are one of the most glamorous couples of American sport. Together, they appeared on the cover of *ESPN Magazine's Body Issue*, and Megan was the first openly homosexual sportswoman to be featured in the pages of the glossy *Sports Illustrated Swimsuit Issue*.

With her bright pink hair and athletic build, she is part of the new group of ambassadors for Victoria's Secret: they are not angels with perfect bodies anymore, but rather women on the front line against discrimination, with no wings but with their feet firmly on the ground. "We have to be better. We have to love more, hate less. We got to listen more and talk less. We got to know this is everybody's responsibility to make this world a better place," said Megan during the touching speech she gave at the FIFA Awards, using words that had never been heard before at an award ceremony. She spoke about homophobia and racism, but also of the wonderful variety of her team. "We have pink hair, purple hair, we have tattoos, dreadlocks. We've got Black girls and White girls. Straight girls, gay girls. It's my absolute honor to lead this team out on the field." With her heart in her hand but her eyes focused on what is really needed to make a difference, Megan chose to break down gender inequalities, putting a spotlight on something that is certainly bigger than a ball rolling into a net.

DANICA ROEM

With her example, the first transgender candidate to be elected in the United States reminds everyone that politics can and must be open to people of any kind. "It doesn't matter what you look like, where you come from, how you worship, who you love."

There are women who, through their daily gestures, political commitment, and striving toward freedom, become the best face of the countries they represent, women like Danica Roem. A photo portrays her on her knees, her face in her hands, crying. It was 2017, and she had just become the first openly transgender congresswoman to be elected in the United States. It was a historic achievement, considering that she was a candidate in Virginia, where her opponent was ultraconservative and had been in that position for twenty-six years. Hers was a personal but also social victory, which involved the whole transgender community.

YOU SHOULD BE CELEBRATED BECAUSE OF WHO YOU ARE, NOT DESPITE IT.

As soon as her victory became official, Danica said: "We made history tonight," speaking to "every person who's ever been singled out, stigmatized, who's ever been the kid in the corner."

"This election has to prove nationwide that discrimination is a disqualifier. This is also your America; this is our shared wealth." Before that day, few people would have bet on her, and when she decided to run for that position, Danica was well aware that for her it was going to be an uphill battle. "There has never been an openly transgender lawmaker in American history. It's not something common. I am the first openly transgender candidate to participate in Virginia. It never happened before, so I have no example to follow." She relentlessly ran her campaign door-to-door and through public appearances, interviews, and constant activity on social media. She always introduced herself by telling her own story with transparency, but without ever using it as a flag.

"Being trans influences my worldview, but it wasn't my qualification to run for office. My qualification was the ten and a half years I spent as a professional news reporter," she told the *New York Times*. "What person is going to be more qualified to represent their community than a lifelong resident of that community who spent their career actually covering the public policy issues of the community?"

Reelected in 2020, Danica keeps fighting for social equality. Her speeches to delegates are always passionate and highlight the change that the recent elections triggered with regard to civil rights. A mission she had always had since her historic election in Virginia, so much so that she dedicated her victory to everyone who, like her, had ever been unjustly marginalized. "To every person who's ever been singled out, who's ever been stigmatized, who's ever been the misfit, who's ever been the kid in the corner, who's ever never had someone to stand up for them because they didn't have a voice of their own, this one's for you."

MARJANE SATRAPI

Raised in Tehran during the revolution, she shared her story with millions of readers with a graphic novel that with courage and irony tells of life under the ayatollah regime in all its nuances. After all, the world is never all black or white, not even in comic strips.

With her brown hair and passionate eyes, Marjane Satrapi has always lived between two cultures, juggling the contradictions. Raised in Iran, she then relocated in Paris. At the age of nine, she used to leaf through Che Guevara's works, at ten years old she had already read *Wuthering Heights*, and at eleven she started reading Sartre's philosophical essays. "If I were a man, I would say that Iran is my mother, and France my wife." She cannot return to her homeland since she published *Persepolis*, the autobiographical graphic novel that made her known all over the world. Released in 2000, it remained among the top-selling books for years and, according to the *Guardian*, it is one of the hundred most representative books of this century.

THE REAL **WAR** IS NOT BETWEEN THE **WEST** AND THE **EAST**. THE REAL **WAR** IS BETWEEN **INTELLIGENT** AND **STUPID PEOPLE**.

The odyssey of the little Iranian girl who plays at being a revolutionary and dreams of becoming a prophet has been translated into more than forty languages and its film adaptation won an Oscar. Inspired by Marjane's childhood in Tehran in the early 1980s during the dictatorship, *Persepolis* is moving and hilarious at the same time. After all, as she herself says, "I wouldn't have survived without humor. I think that irony is a matter of intelligence." Still today, it is considered a controversial book. And indeed, wearing a jacket that says "Punk is not dead" over a chador as Marjane did when she was a teenager is a really powerful transgression, a courageous challenge, and a cry for freedom. In the introduction of *Persepolis*, she writes: "I believe that an entire nation should not be judged by the wrongdoings of a few extremists. I also don't want those Iranians who lost their lives in prisons defending freedom, who died in the war against Iraq, who suffered under various repressive regimes, or who were forced to leave their families and flee their homeland to be forgotten. One can forgive but one should never forget."

With her black-and-white drawings, she managed to trigger a small cultural revolution in Western mentality by showing the hidden side of this story and by strongly denouncing the machismo and fundamentalism that turned the social and family life of millions of women into a tyranny. Marjane was considered one of the most famous contemporary cartoonists, but only for a little while. After she created *Embroideries* and *Chicken with Plums*, two spin-offs of her masterpiece, she moved on. She is now dedicating herself to painting, and colors have appeared: red, blue, and green illuminate her minimalist portraits of women lost and suspended in their thoughts. A world of women that Marjane recounts through cinema as well. As a director and screenwriter, she has no doubt as to where to put the spotlight. "Women in cinema often play the role of somebody's mother, somebody's sister, or somebody's lover. They must be sweet and gentle. It's the result of centuries of patriarchy and it will take time to change it. We are half of the world population in numbers, so it would be very normal that our stories would be half of the stories."

CULTURE AND EDUCATION ARE THE LETHAL WEAPONS AGAINST ALL KINDS OF FUNDAMENTALISM.

ALICE SCHWARZER

Fiery and passionate, she fought historic battles in the name of women's freedom. Yesterday as today, the leader of the feminist movement in Germany remains faithful to the motto that accompanied every moment of her life: "I will think, write, and act as long as I live."

Alice has always had the gift of attracting attention. Some people consider her the living icon of the struggle for female empowerment, while for some others she is "die Hexe," the witch: the prototype of the intransigent activist who hates the masculine gender. Nevertheless, no one denies that she was and still is the embodiment of the feminist movement in Germany. Incapable of accepting compromises, strong-willed, and always driven by tenacity and coherence, she has never shied away from pushing her feminist battles to the limit. It can be said that she has been a rebel since her birth, given that she is the daughter of a twenty-three-year-old unmarried mother in Nazi Germany, where the law forced single

WOMEN ARE NO LONGER SATISFIED WITH HALF OF THE SKY; THEY WANT HALF OF THE WORLD.

mothers to give their illegitimate children to the Führer so that they could be raised in an institution.

Her family opposed this law and Alice grew up in her maternal grandparents' home, with a "caring grandfather and a politically active grandmother." As soon as she was able to, she fled from an oppressive reality to move to the city of her dreams, Paris, where she lived by her wits, but she could enjoy freedom and a lively atmosphere. She met the writer Simone de Beauvoir and found herself in the middle of the upheaval triggered by the French feminist movement. When she came back, she knew exactly what she was going to do: she would become a journalist and bring that breath of freedom also in her own country. Her first revolutionary act was to convince the magazine *Stern* to take a public pro-abortion stand. In total, 374 photos of women who admitted they had an abortion, including illustrious actresses like Romy Schneider and Senta Berger, were published in the June 6, 1971, issue. In the '70s, the name of Alice Schwarzer was on everyone's lips, and she finally had the chance to pull off the even more ambitious challenge of creating and running a magazine that reflected her worldview. The magazine *Emma*, created in 1977, became a relentless observatory that closely follows and analyzes all the most important events from a feminist point of view. With her magazine, Alice launched her historical battles for equal salary and rights, but also against domestic violence, misogynist cover images, offensive advertisement, and pornography. Acute, combative, and controversial, she was often criticized, and she even ended up on a collision course with feminists. Over time, the turmoil seemed to subside. Alice became a familiar face on the most popular television shows, and Germany was relieved to realize that the polemicist of the past was not so dangerous after all. So much so that Alice was awarded one of the highest national honors, the Bundesverdienstkreuz, the German Federal Cross of Merit. Yesterday as today, women owe her a great deal. "Our daughters owe feminists like me an equal legal position, even within marriage, and a world within reach—at least in theory. Our sons, on the other hand, have to thank us for not having to be machos anymore but just men." Alice is aware that we are still far from the ultimate goal. "After all, a patriarchy of at least 5,000 years will certainly not be abolished in fifty years." But she does not give up, always faithful to the motto that accompanied every moment of her life: "I will think, write, and act as long as I live."

THE **ENGINE** DRIVING EVERYTHING
I DO IS **FAIRNESS.**
ANYTHING **ELSE** WOULD HAVE, FOR ME,
BEEN A MISUSE OF MY **LIFE.**

JULIE SWEET

Visionariness, charisma, and constant leadership even in uncertain times are the elements that took her to the top of Fortune's *ranking, which rewards the most powerful women in the business world. She now uses her influence to eradicate discrimination and teach women to dream big.*

Her motto is engraved on a plaque that her husband gave her: "If your dreams don't scare you, they aren't big enough." She has made it her lifestyle, aiming for the top without being afraid of dealing with her weaknesses, even if she is one of the most powerful women in the world, according to *Fortune*'s ranking. Julie is the CEO of the global consulting firm Accenture and the first woman to hold this post in a multinational company with half a million employees. And yet, she is not afraid of being totally transparent, because, according to her, frankness is one of the most important values for a leader.

DIVERSITY
IS CRITICAL
TO INNOVATION.

She proved it during a speech she gave in front of young MBA students at the University of Texas, when she could not hold back her emotion in recalling how hard it had been for her to make a career in a male environment. "I committed in that moment that I would make it better for the women coming after me," she pointed out. She uncompromisingly carries on her commitment to promoting diversity in gender, race, sexual orientation, and any other kind of differences, with the belief that it is also beneficial for the profits. When, in 2015, she became CEO of Accenture North America, she set as a goal to hire 40 percent women, and to achieve gender equality among all employees. The first woman to lead this consulting giant, she built her fortune on her own, coming from a very humble beginning. Born and raised in Tustin, California, she remembers that as a young girl she only had one pair of trousers and one pair of shoes, because her parents used to buy her new ones only when she grew a size. She started working when she was fourteen at a theater booking office to pay for her own clothes. "I realized early on that I needed to go against the flow and be better than everyone else to support my family," she told the *Huffington Post*.

She has never been afraid to explore uncharted territories to stand out. And so, she chose to study Mandarin at college, and she went to live in Beijing and Taiwan for a year. "That experience gave me tremendous confidence," she recalls. After graduation, she was hired as a business lawyer by Cravath, Swaine & Moore, Wall Street's most prestigious law firm. There were very few women, and Julie took advantage of this lack of diversity to stand out: "There were not a lot of women in any room I was in. So, when you're good, you stand out." When, at the age of forty-three, as a mother of two girls and already a successful woman, she received a call from a recruiter offering her a job in Accenture, Julie accepted without a second thought. Her imperatives are never stop studying, being curious, and keeping up to date. She is strongly engaged in inclusion-related issues, and in response to the murders of George Floyd, Ahmaud Arbery, and Breonna Taylor, she publicly came out against racism, hate, and every kind of violence and discrimination, reaffirming her commitment to a fairer society, with more job and advancement opportunities for everyone, especially for women.

HAVE THE **CONFIDENCE** TO **FOCUS ON UNCHARTED** **TERRITORY.** TAKE **CHANCES.**

GRETA THUNBERG

After the memorable speech she gave in front of UN representatives, she became the most famous environmental activist in the world. Beyond slogans and controversies, she has never stopped involving young people, with the certainty that the environment must remain the priority.

Every Friday, a fifteen-year-old Swedish girl, instead of going to school, decided to sit in front of the Stockholm Riksdag to strike against the government's lack of interest in the face of the risks of climate change. She held a sign that read "Skolstrejk för klimatet," meaning "school strike for the climate." Less than a year later, her face, framed by braids under the hood of a yellow raincoat, appeared on magazine covers worldwide. Greta became the symbol of the fight to protect the environment, and her Fridays for Future movement reached a global scope, so much so that on September 20, 2019, it gave rise to the first and largest Global Climate Strike in history, supported by four million people in 161 countries.

WE NEED TO **WALK** THE **TALK**—IF WE DO THIS **TOGETHER,** WE CAN DO THIS.

Greta did not stop, and at the UN climate summit she addressed a memorable and very tough speech to the leaders gathered in front of her. "You have stolen my dreams and my childhood with your empty words. And yet I'm one of the lucky ones. People are suffering. People are dying. Entire ecosystems are collapsing. We are in the beginning of a mass extinction, and all you can talk about is money and fairy tales of eternal economic growth. How dare you! This is all wrong. I shouldn't be up here. I should be back in school on the other side of the ocean. Yet, you all come to us young people for hope. How dare you!" At the age of sixteen, the champion for the environment was on the cover of *Time* and spoke at the World Economic Forum in Switzerland, reminding everyone that the world economy must be deeply rethought for the sake of the environment. Despite having Asperger syndrome ("I wouldn't say that I suffer from it; let's say that I have it," she specifies), Greta never stops traveling around the world, strictly by train or boat, to meet leading figures. Loved and hated, she has undoubtedly left her mark.

The impact that this teenager has had on public opinion has been so radical that today it would be impossible to imagine the ecological struggle without Greta. She is the symbol of an urgent and necessary fight for the survival of the entire planet, and an example followed by millions of young people who, like her, believe that adults are not able to look at the present, let alone the future. "I don't want your hope. I want you to panic," she told the leaders gathered at the Davos World Economic Forum. "I want you to feel the fear I feel every day. Our house is on fire. But there is still time to turn everything around." Her greatest merit is that she brought the issue to the surface, finally stirring consciences. As *Time* wrote, "Meaningful change rarely happens without the galvanizing force of influential individuals, and the Earth's existential crisis found one in Greta Thunberg."

I HAVE LEARNED THAT YOU ARE NEVER TOO SMALL TO MAKE A DIFFERENCE.

BEBE VIO

She is the winner of the Paralympic foil gold medal and brand ambassador for Dior, and she was even guest of honor at the White House. With her armor, this champion can win any challenge with a charming smile and an unshakable confidence in the value of diversity: "Be special."

At the age of twenty-four, Bebe has already achieved it all: Olympic gold medal, World Cup, and European Championships. She was awarded a Laureus Award (the sports version of the Oscars), she has more than a million enthusiastic followers on Instagram, she published two books to tell her story, she had dinner with Barack Obama, and she walked the catwalk for Dior. All of this without ever losing sight of what really matters because, as she says, "if you don't have a family that loves and supports you, you're nothing." Loved and supported, she has really become someone, overcoming extremely difficult challenges. Fond of fencing since her childhood, when she was eleven years old, Bebe was affected by severe meningitis, which forced doctors to amputate her arms and legs to keep her alive.

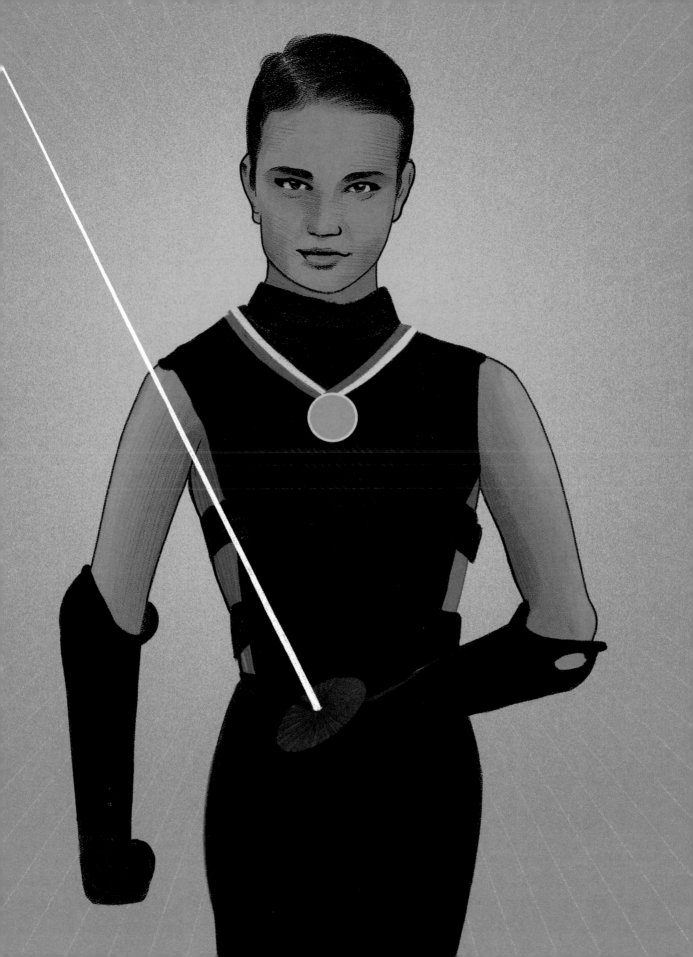

IF IT SEEMS IMPOSSIBLE, THEN IT CAN BE DONE.

"When I was a kid, I was told that I could not fence without my arms, and that I had to play a different sport, but I proved to everyone that you don't need arms for it: if you have a dream, go and get it," she said during the Paralympics opening ceremony. With the energy and determination of a superhero, she faced the challenge of rehabilitation without hesitation. Thanks to the prosthesis that her father designed for her, Bebe has become the first athlete in the world to use an armed prosthesis on which to insert the foil. With determination, sacrifice, enthusiasm, and an endless series of exhausting workouts, she managed to achieve the objective she had always had since her childhood: the gold medal at the Rio de Janeiro Paralympics. Since that moment, Bebe has not stopped pursuing her dream, proving that with passion and willpower you can do everything you want. "Her story is one of rising against all odds. She is the image of her generation, a leader and advocate for the causes she believes in. And she has managed to achieve all of that by living up to her belief that if it seems impossible, then it can be done," said Ursula Von der Leyen while introducing the Italian athlete to the European Parliament in Strasbourg.

"For me resilience is the spirit of adaptability," said Bebe, encouraging everyone to look at diversity in the right way, just as she did, gaining strength from her weaknesses to foster her great love of life. In order to support those who find themselves in the same situation, she founded Art4sport with the help of her parents, an association that helps child amputees to integrate into society through sport. Her dream is now to have sporting events free from psychological or physical barriers, where athletes can all compete on the same field because, as she says, "with or without disabilities, sports make everyone believe that everything is possible." This is a certainty she continues to assert without fear and with a self-awareness that makes her irresistible. That's why she refuses to cover the scars on her face with makeup. Those markings are part of her, just as her green eyes and her wonderful smile.

PEOPLE OFTEN GIVE UP IN THE FACE OF DIFFICULTIES, BUT YOU ALWAYS HAVE TO BELIEVE IN YOUR DREAMS.

KARA WALKER

With her art she denounces the horrors of slavery, filtering them through the shadows of black silhouettes dancing on the walls of museums. Thanks to her, African American art acquired great visibility after having been neglected for a long time.

Cut out of paper and wax-glued to the walls, the black-and-white figures created by Kara Walker catch the eye with their seductive elegance, but then they nail it with the harshness of the stories they tell, imbued with racism and violence. The silhouettes of slaves and masters evoke the horrors of the Southern slave states, tearing apart the sugary atmospheres of *Uncle Tom's Cabin* and *Gone with the Wind*. If you look at them carefully, you will notice that these delicate images reveal a sequence of abuse, murders, and subjugation set in rural sceneries hidden behind the landscapes of cotton plantations.

IF YOU'RE A BLACK ARTIST, YOU COULD PAINT A WALL OF SMILING FACES, AND SOMEONE WILL STILL ASK YOU: "WHY ARE YOU SO ANGRY?"

These figures play on the contrast between form and content to tell the story of a feudal world populated by rich and poor, Black and White people, men and animals. Here, the roles of power are continuously reshuffled through sex, which in Kara's works is often brutal, with no barriers of gender or age. Kara moves on the thin line between what must be denounced and what one does not dare say. She herself is torn between the temptation to be identified as an anti-racist icon and that of avoiding exposure. She prefers not to be classified as an African American artist, or as a female artist, thus avoiding all stereotypes. "I do not speak for all women, but for myself, and even that with difficulty. The only key is my psyche, there is no feminist key," she said.

The daughter of an artist, Kara took as a role model her father, who taught her how to redress and neutralize a history of racial and social injustice in her works. Cultivated and charismatic, she debuted in the early '90s, and she soon achieved international fame. At the age of twenty-eight, Kara was honored with the MacArthur Fellowship, a $500,000 prestigious prize also known as the "Genius

Grant" because it is awarded to between twenty and thirty Americans who have shown extraordinary creativity in their work.

Her works were purchased by the MoMA and exhibited in great solo exhibitions at the Whitney Museum in New York, the Tate Modern in London, and the Apartheid Museum in Johannesburg. Over the years, she added to the black cutouts on white backgrounds not only shadow puppet theaters inspired by the Javanese tradition and magic-lantern projections, but also videos with figures moved like puppets by her hands shot in grainy 16-millimeter, like vintage short films. Kara's constant experimentation always arouses a very strong emotional response in viewers, which is provoked by the mix of the visual elegance of her works, the atrocities they depict, and a cynical sense of humor. To whoever asks her what she thinks about the fact that viewers might feel upset, she relentlessly answers: "You can decide to look at my work or not. In my head, the whole range of images of Black people is a free reign. Their intent is not to fascinate a racist. What I want is for viewers to deal with their own prejudices, desires, and fears."

CLARISSA WARD

She is one of the most famous and courageous journalists in the world. The English Clarissa Ward, a CNN correspondent in Kabul, captured tragic and upsetting images to let the world know the truth.

She coldly and courageously documented the descent into hell of a nation occupied by the Taliban by recounting those days that rewrote the history of Afghanistan, from the American withdrawal to the fall of Kabul and the chaos at the airport, where desperate mothers gave their children to soldiers in order to save them. With great professionalism, and without ever showing a moment of weariness, Clarissa has shown the world the powerful effects of a journalist capable of telling the facts through the power of images. Then, she had to give up because staying in Kabul had become too dangerous for those like her, who had faced the Taliban with their face uncovered.

WE HAVE AN **ADVANTAGE** COMPARED TO MEN. WE CAN **SPEAK** WITH **WOMEN**, WHO ARE **GOLD MINES** OF **INFORMATION**.

"Cover yourself!" they shouted at her on the street, waving their Kalashnikovs and making it extremely clear what their idea of women, especially career women, was. A few seconds later, the crew was assaulted in an attempt to seize their cameras. Her reaction in that moment of great danger was exemplary: she replied with a calm, low, and gentle voice, as if she was not surrounded by men armed to their teeth. "If they do that to me, can you imagine what they can do to Afghans?" she said. She has never been afraid of putting herself at risk to tell the world the truth of even the most brutal and violent facts. "I was initially driven to do this work because of 9/11, which happened my senior year at Yale. I just was really struggling to understand how something like this could happen and how there could be such a fundamental lack of communication in the world," she said in an interview. Born in London to an American mother and a British father, she collaborated with American television media giants such as ABC, CBS, and Fox. With her reportages, she recounted the Israeli-Palestinian conflict, the Syrian civil war, and the Ukrainian revolution.

She made reportages about important events such as the capture of Saddam Hussein, the 2004 tsunami in the Indian Ocean, and the deaths of Yasser Arafat and Pope John Paul II. She was awarded the Peabody Award, and she became famous for traveling in Syria disguised as a tourist with a hidden camera, getting in touch with rebel groups to film and interview them. Being a woman never made her feel weak. On the contrary, she believes that women war correspondents have a great advantage. "As a woman, I have access to 50 percent of the population that my male counterparts don't have access to, and women are gold mines of information." When asked why she chooses to be dressed as local women instead of wearing Western clothes, she frankly answers: "For my security. In Syria, you will see me almost always wearing an abaya and hijab. That's primarily because I could be kidnapped if people knew that I was a Western journalist. But it's also because nobody looks twice at me when I wear that, and there's something extremely liberating about that." In TV studios she always appears elegant and feminine, even if her true nature is being out in the field, as she herself admits: "I feel more comfortable in combat boots and a flak jacket."

MY JOB IS TO GET OUT ON THE STREETS AND HEAR WHAT PEOPLE ARE THINKING AND SEE WHAT'S GOING ON.

EMMA WATSON

Her magic potion is a mix of beauty, personality, and commitment. This is how this young star became a UN ambassador, a leading figure in the fight for women's rights, and a champion for ethical fashion.

The world first knew her with a magic wand in her hand, in the Harry Potter saga, but Emma has never been an actress like the others. With a typically British elegance (even if she was born in Paris), behind her sweetness she hides an iron, top-of-the-class-like character. With her resoluteness and determined gaze, she earned fame by playing Hermione, but then the spell was broken. She built up her powerful identity through other blockbusters, such as *Beauty and the Beast*, and a slew of art films from Sofia Coppola's *Bling Ring* to *Little Women*. However, Emma does not just look for new challenges on set, as she demonstrated when she put her career on hold to devote herself to her studies, graduating in English literature from the prestigious Brown University in the United States.

I AM **INVITING** YOU TO **STEP FORWARD**, TO BE SEEN, **SPEAK UP.** AND TO ASK YOURSELF IF NOT ME, **WHO?** IF NOT NOW, **WHEN?**

But it was still not enough for her. "I want to be a Renaissance woman. I want to paint, and I want to write, and I want to act, and I just want to do everything," she told herself. And so, she dove right in to social and political commitments. She strongly supports several humanitarian causes, such as the Time's Up movement, demonstrating her commitment with concrete actions, like when she donated a million pounds to a British association for women victims of harassment and abuse at work. She was appointed Goodwill ambassador for gender equality by the UN, and she never missed an opportunity to urge men to become allies of women in their fight toward a true equality. "I want men to take up this mantle," she said. She explained what the role of men should be in promoting gender equality when, during the #HeforShe campaign, she asked: "How can we effect change in the world when only half of it is invited or feels welcome to participate in the conversation?" Then, she directly addressed men while speaking about those stereotypes that they should be the first to break down. They should do this "so their daughters, sisters, and mothers can be free from prejudice but also so that their sons have permission to be vulnerable." She expressed her stance without hesitation when she spoke to the United Nations. "I have realized that fighting for women's rights has too often become synonymous with man-hating. If there is one thing I know for certain, it is that this has to stop. For the record, feminism by definition is the belief that men and women should have equal rights and opportunities. It is the theory of the political, economic, and social equality of the sexes." Her speech was greeted by a standing ovation and went viral, so much so that Malala Yousafzai said in an interview that she became a feminist right after listening to Emma's words. Alongside the social commitment, this undeniably charming actress proves to have a green soul by wearing fully sustainable dresses on the red carpet to show that a different fashion is possible. Sensitive and resolute, the young witch has grown up, but she has not lost her magic wand. On the contrary, she now uses it to uphold the ideals of a generation of young women who are increasingly committed and attentive to ethics and sustainability.

BETHANY WILLIAMS

Pioneer of sustainability, she designs colored and unisex clothes manufactured with organic materials and fabric scraps. Hers is an ethical commitment to the environment and to vulnerable people because fashion, too, can change lives.

Ethical, inclusive, handmade fashion that gives value to principles like frankness, kindness, care, and dignity, and that sees scraps as raw materials with which to create a beautiful story: this is Bethany's brilliant project. She is the queen of sustainability and upcycling, and she has been awarded by another queen, the Queen of England, with the Queen Elizabeth II Award for British Design. Selected for the LVMH Prize, she was awarded the NewGen award by the British Fashion Council. She also won the British Emerging Talent Menswear at the Fashion Awards, and the Vogue Talents 10. She was deservedly showered with awards intended for emerging talents who stand out for their originality, eco-sustainability,

FASHION HAS THE ABILITY TO AMPLIFY IDEAS AND TAKE THEM TO A BIGGER STAGE.

and sensitiveness to social issues. And indeed, no one is able to combine all these elements in such an extraordinary way like she does.

Her ascent coincided with a radical change in the fashion world, which has finally started taking climate and social issues seriously. "I was really interested in sustainability growing up. My mum is very hot on environmental issues; I've always been around these ideas."

Convinced that fashion can become an engine for social change, she does not only manufacture her collections with recycled materials, but she also involves charities. Just as she did with her 2019 fashion show, which she called "Adelaide House," a tribute to the Liverpool halfway house for women victims of domestic violence, ex-convicts, and homeless. The clothes were manufactured with recycled paper obtained from wax-coated strips of newspapers woven like yarn and decorated with Liverpool urban landscapes and portraits of women from Adelaide House. Two years later, she presented a collection of coats made with recycled vintage blankets, because everything in her manufacturing process is 100 percent sustainable, even buttons, which are hand-carved from branches of silver birches sustainably grown in the Lake District. The decorations are handled by the Max Workshop for the Disabled, on the Isle of Man, which helps people who have physical or mental disabilities with work. The fabrics are made by women inmates from the Downview prison or by the Italian San Patrignano community, which deals with the rehabilitation of drug addicts. "When the girls from these realities see something they have handwoven in *Vogue*, it gives them encouragement and confidence which is really needed in order for them to progress," explains Bethany. Her collections are intentionally oversize, and tend to be unisex, even if they are primarily intended for the menswear market. "I like the idea that if a man supports or buys the collection in store, he's helping to fund all these projects we do with women. It's feminist whether you're doing it consciously or unconsciously." With her project, Bethany proved that an alternative fashion production system does exist, which is more ethical and with no shortcuts. "I do like to have a social benefit through my work. Growing a business in a sustainable way is difficult but definitely worth it."

OPRAH WINFREY

She is a talk show host, actress, producer, businesswoman, and philanthropist who built her career on her overwhelming personality. Rich, powerful, and generous, she is the embodiment of the American dream, and perhaps even more than that.

She achieved so many records throughout her life that no one can hold a candle to her. Nevertheless, her recognitions and earnings take a back seat to the social and cultural impact that this extraordinary woman has had on society. The elements of Oprah's exceptional winning formula include empathy and a genuine interest in social and cultural issues, which she sees as a way to improve herself through altruism. "I love what I do. I have suffered a lot in my life, but all of this has shaped me and made me stronger. And above all it helped me understand others and their problems. I have always had a fondness for the disadvantaged classes, and I feel a deep need to dedicate my life to helping others."

I WAS RAISED TO **BELIEVE** THAT **EXCELLENCE** IS THE BEST **DETERRENT** TO **RACISM** OR **SEXISM**. AND THAT'S HOW I OPERATE **MY LIFE**.

Hers is a story of revenge that starts in Mississippi, where she was born and raised in extreme poverty. Abused and mistreated, Oprah redeemed herself thanks to her studies and her ability to make herself heard. Charismatic since she was a teenager, she started out in Nashville's churches by reciting the poems of James Weldon Johnson, a pioneer in the fight for African American civil rights. She then moved on to radio, and by the age of twenty she was already a TV news anchor. She felt so at ease in front of the cameras that she was given the possibility to host her own talk show, which was very risky in a period when almost all the TV hosts were white men. *The Oprah Winfrey Show* debuted in 1986, and from that moment on she took her career in her own hands. She addressed issues such as violence against women, drugs, and social problems, disclosing her own life stories. The audience appreciated her honesty, her strength, and her ability to talk transparently. Oprah became one of America's most influential women and she set audience records, like in 1993, when she interviewed Michael Jackson in front of 100 million viewers. Twenty-five years after the first episode, Oprah ended her talk show to become a businesswoman with her own network.

She also managed to fulfill her childhood dream of becoming an actress. She won applause for her performances in Steven Spielberg's *The Color Purple* and in *Selma*, with an Oscar nomination for both of them. Powerful and rich, Oprah never stops helping the less fortunate because she knows what it means to suffer. For her, even motherhood is related to a painful episode. She was abused when she was little more than a child and she gave birth to a premature baby who did not survive. Since then, she never became pregnant again. For many years now, however, she has been taking care of the girls of the Leadership Academy, her college in Johannesburg, South Africa. "Love knows no boundaries. It doesn't matter if a child came from your womb or if you found that person at age two, ten, or twenty." Her effort is so huge that the President of the United States Barack Obama awarded her the Presidential Medal of Freedom, the greatest civil honor. For the new generations, she is an icon of equal rights for all cultures, races, and genders.

SUCCESS IS THE BEST REVENGE.

MALALA YOUSAFZAI

By shooting her in her head, fundamentalists wanted to shut her up forever, but they instead turned her into a superstar. After graduating from Oxford, she continued to promote girls' rights to education with her Malala Fund and a very special book club.

Can a little girl change the world? Malala Yousafzai did that when she was little more than a child. She became the symbol of the struggle for young people's right to education all over the world. With the courage and boldness of a warrior, she opposed the Taliban, which in Pakistan had taken control of schools, limiting access to education, and she openly challenged them. "How dare they take away my right to education?" she asked herself in the posts she used to write for the BBC, documenting the living conditions of children under the regime. She was only eleven, and her activism caused a great stir, but also inevitably attracted the fury of the Taliban, who decreed her death sentence.

I KNOW THE POWER THAT A YOUNG GIRL CARRIES IN HER HEART WHEN SHE HAS A VISION AND A MISSION.

It seemed impossible that someone could really lash out against a child, but on October 9, 2012, something unimaginable happened: they shot her in her head while she was leaving school. Her iron character and an endless series of surgeries helped her get back on her feet. On her sixteenth birthday, her voice resounded in the UN General Assembly Hall, where she gave a moving speech in front of Secretary-General Ban Ki-moon, the delegates, and four hundred young people. "Let us pick up our books and our pens; they are the most powerful weapons. One child, one teacher, one book, and one pen can change the world." While she was speaking, Malala knew that the Taliban had vowed vengeance, but she has always stated that she is not afraid anymore: "They thought a bullet would silence us, but they failed. Nothing changed in my life except this: Weaknesses, fear, and hopelessness died. Strength, power, and courage was born." According to Malala, the tables ended up turning and now, she says, the Taliban are the ones who are afraid of her: "The power of education frightens them. They are afraid of women. And that is why they kill: because they were, and they are afraid."

Instead of eliminating her, they turned her into the most powerful voice against oppression: an epic fail, as it is said in social media slang. Her courage was awarded with the Nobel Peace Prize in 2014. Malala was seventeen when she became the youngest winner of this prestigious prize. She became a UN Messenger of Peace with the task of promoting female schooling. One year later, she celebrated her eighteenth birthday with the opening of a school for Syrian refugees in Lebanon, and she then enrolled at Oxford University. "Now I am able to study at a prestigious university—but I want to live in a world where every girl is able to weigh her future career options." After graduating with honors, the author of the bestseller *I Am Malala* did certainly not sit back doing nothing. In addition to constantly promoting education everywhere in the world with her Malala Fund, she decided to start her very personal book club, which she called Fearless. "Together we'll explore books from new voices and prominent writers—women with bold ideas and storytellers who show the world from their unique perspective," she said on Instagram. What could be more poetic than feminism explained by a woman like her?

CHLOÉ ZHAO

Born in China but educated in the United States, Chloé is applauded worldwide. By drawing a thin line between sentiment and sentimentalism, she is rewriting the history of cinema with her movies. From the Golden Lion to the Oscar, she won it all.

It took her a while to understand that cinema was her vocation, but she soon made up for lost time. Now that she has taken flight, no one can stop her. In less than five years, she collected an impressive number of awards, and she won the Oscar before being hired by Marvel to direct a cast of superheroes. The most highly acclaimed director in the world is a petite woman, born and raised in Beijing. At school she was a nuisance, and she preferred manga to textbooks. She was obsessed with Western culture, from MTV to movies such as *Terminator* and *Sister Act*, so much so that her parents decided to support her by sending her to study in a college in London when she was fourteen. One step away from her diploma, she told her parents she wanted to go "where the Hollywood sign is" and transferred to Los Angeles.

PEOPLE AT **BIRTH** ARE INHERENTLY **GOOD. I** STILL TRULY BELIEVE IT TODAY. I HAVE ALWAYS FOUND **GOODNESS** IN THE PEOPLE I MET **EVERYWHERE** I WENT IN THE **WORLD.**

"I knew so little about America. Michael Jordan, Michael Jackson, Madonna, Prince—that's all I really cared about. I was pretty ignorant. But when you drop me in downtown LA in 1999, there's a lot to discover," she said while recounting her first impression of the United States. She would never leave the United States, after having fallen under the spell of Western landscapes, which became the background of her road movie *Nomadland*, a portrait of those itinerant American communities that travel by camper, odd-jobbing. It is a sensitive and moving analysis, filmed as a documentary with real people, with the exception of the protagonist Frances McDormand. Critically acclaimed, this movie made Chloé the first Asian and the second woman (after Kathryn Bigelow with *The Hurt Locker*) to be awarded the Oscar for Best Director in the history of the Academy Awards. It is a remarkable achievement, and it is even more striking considering that Chloé had only directed two movies before this masterpiece.

After several precarious jobs, when she was thirty-five, she filmed her first feature film, *Songs My Brothers Taught Me*, a story of rebellion and brotherhood filmed on an Indian reservation in South Dakota and presented at the Sundance Film Festival.

Two years later, she was awarded the Art Cinema Award in Cannes for the movie *Rider*. Both movies were low-budget independent movies inspired by Chloé's reporter instincts and filmed after infiltrating the communities that captured her interest from time to time. "I want to continue to work that way in the future, whether it's a bigger film or a smaller film. Because I always find people are just so interesting." At the Oscars, she appeared onstage with two long braids and white sneakers. She thanked her colleagues and the whole cast, and she dedicated her victory to "anyone who had the faith and courage to hold on to the goodness in themselves and to hold on in the goodness in each other no matter how difficult it is to do that." That award made her famous intellectually, but the commercial success came with *Eternals*, which made her the first Chinese American world-class filmmaker. A champion of indie film, the director gives her superheroes a feminist, inclusive, and definitely innovative twist. Chloé is a powerful anecdote against any kind of cultural barrier.

TOO OFFEN WE FORGET TO ADMIRE THE EARTH, ONLY TO FEEL IT UNDER OUR FEET.

Chiara Pasqualetti Johnson. A journalist from Milan, Chiara graduated in art history, and writes about travel, art, and lifestyle for major Italian magazines. She edited books and series about modern and contemporary art history for publishers Electa and Rizzoli. With White Star Publishers she published, in 2018, *The Most Influential Women of Our Time*, an illustrated volume dedicated to the most influential female figures of the twentieth century and translated into twelve languages. In 2020, *Coco Chanel. Revolutionary Woman*, a bestseller issued in five international editions, was published followed by *Chanel N°5. The Perfume of the Century*, dedicated to the most famous perfume in the world, and *Breakfast at Audrey's*. In 2021 Chiara was included by Forbes Italy among the 100 Wonder Women of the year, successful women united by winning leadership and creativity.

Alessandro Ventrella was born in Castellaneta (Province of Taranto). In 2015 he began his academic studies in graphic design at the Accademia di Belle Arti in Macerata, and then at the CFP Bauer in Milan (2018-2020), where he also attended his first course of Illustration. From that moment on, his passion for drawing also became his job. His drawings often depict personalities from the show business who played an important role in his personal growth. His illustrations are sometimes very detailed and sometimes reduced to essentials. He currently works in Milan as illustrator and graphic designer.

Project Editor and Editorial Supervison
Valeria Manferto De Fabianis

Graphic design
Maria Cucchi

WHITE STAR PUBLISHERS

WS White Star Publishers® is a registered trademark property of White Star s.r.l.

© 2022 White Star s.r.l.
Piazzale Luigi Cadorna, 6
20123 Milan, Italy
www.whitestar.it

Translation: Carlotta Cappato – Editing: Abby Young

Copyright © 2022 by Chiara Pasqualetti Johnson. Published by Mango Publishing, a division of Mango Publishing Group, Inc.

Library of Congress Cataloging-in-Publication number: Has been requested
ISBN: (print) 978-1-68481-034-5,
\(ebook) 978-1-68481-035-2
BISAC category code BISAC:
YAN006140YOUNG ADULT NONFICTION /
Biography & Autobiography / Women